His Master's Reflection

Travels with John Polidori,
Lord Byron's Doctor and
Author of The Vampyre

Photo reproduction of a print after a portrait of Lord Byron by Thomas Phillips, anonymous, after Thomas Phillips, *c.* 1870, Rijksmuseum

His Master's Reflection

Travels with John Polidori, Lord Byron's Doctor and Author of The Vampyre

ANDREW AND SUZANNE EDWARDS

sussex
ACADEMIC
PRESS
Brighton • Chicago • Toronto

2 4 6 8 10 9 7 5 3 1

First published in 2019 in Great Britain by
SUSSEX ACADEMIC PRESS
PO Box 139
Eastbourne BN24 9BP

Distributed in North America by
SUSSEX ACADEMIC PRESS
Independent Publishers Group
814 N. Franklin Street, Chicago, IL 60610

British Library Cataloguing in Publication Data
A CIP catalogue record for this book is available from the British Library.

Library of Congress Cataloging-in-Publication Data
Names: Edwards, Andrew (Translator), author. | Edwards, Suzanne, 1967– author.
Title: His master's reflection : travels with John Polidori, Lord Byron's doctor and author of The Vampyre / Andrew and Suzanne Edwards.
Description: Brighton ; Chicago : Sussex Academic Press, 2019. | Includes bibliographical references and index.
Identifiers: LCCN 2018028870 | ISBN 9781845199531 (pbk : acid-free paper)
Subjects: LCSH: Polidori, John William, 1795–1821—Travel. | Byron, George Gordon Byron, Baron, 1788–1824—Friends and associates. | Novelists, English—19th century—Biography. | Physicians—Great Britain—Biography. Polidori, John William, 1795–1821. Vampyre.
Classification: LCC PR5187.P5 Z59 2019 | DDC 823/.7 [B] —dc23
LC record available at https://lccn.loc.gov/2018028870

Typeset & designed by Sussex Academic Press, Brighton & Eastbourne.
Printed by TJ International, Padstow, Cornwall.

Contents

The Illustrations

The cover illustrations are detailed on the back cover.
Frontispiece: Photo reproduction of a print after a portrait of Lord Byron by Thomas Phillips, c. 1870, (anonymous, Rijksmuseum)

The author and publisher gratefully acknowledge permission to repro-
duce copyright material as detailed in the above list. The publishers
apologize for any errors or omissions in the above list and would be
grateful to be notified of any corrections that should be incorporated
in the next edition or reprint of this book.

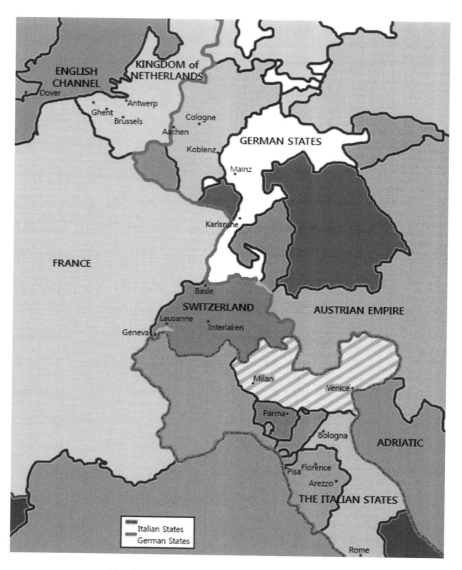

Key locations in the travels of John Polidori

This book is dedicated to
Youth
&
With heartfelt thanks to Franklin Bishop

CHAPTER ONE

Starting Out
The High Road

The first effects were felt as far away as Borneo and Sulawesi with ash beginning to settle on the palms; a portentous precursor to the devastation that would follow. On the island of Sumbawa, Mount Tambora had finally given vent to the unsustainable pressure of magma hidden within its cavernous chambers. Thousands lost their lives in the immediate aftermath of the eruption whilst thousands more in the south-east Asian region would succumb to disease or starve as agricultural output withered to nothing.

Tambora's volcanic outburst in the April of 1815 was of such magnitude that the sheer volume of material hurled into the atmosphere inevitably found its way across continents, lingering in a malignant haze that turned day into night and the summer of 1816 into winter. European hearths were ablaze against the unworldly chill of the July darkness. Around a fireplace in Cologny, on the shores of Lake Geneva, five young friends who should have been strolling under the blanket of a warm alpine evening, were instead forced inside once more by the incessant rain.

Lord Byron stood by the fireside of his rented villa; inspired by the gloom, the poet turned to a book of German tales translated into the French they all understood. This *Fantasmagoriana* captivated his audience — Claire Clairmont, his mistress, already enthralled by her lover, listened in restless awe, as the highly-strung Percy Bysshe Shelley, seated next to his future wife, Mary, became increasingly agitated. Byron then laid down a challenge that has passed into literary history: each of them was to write a ghost story.

Former Polidori residence,
38 Great Pulteney Street,
London, S. Edwards

St Mary's Church, Dover,
A. Edwards

Edinburgh Rooftops, Lino9999, Pixabay

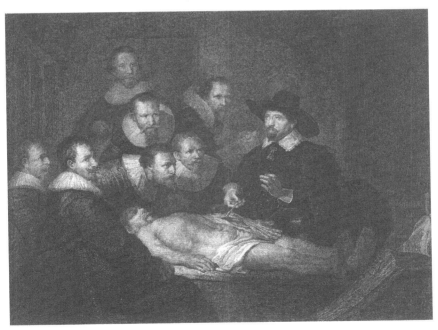

The anatomical lesson of Nicolaes Tulp, Johannes Pieter de Frey, after Rembrandt van Rijn, 1798, Rijksmuseum

On the following evening, the aristocrat continued his readings with Coleridge's poem, *Christabel*. As he evoked Samuel Taylor's image of a witch's wasted breast, Shelley ran from the room screaming. At this alarming juncture, the young, dark-haired doctor who had accompanied Byron to Switzerland, rose to his feet and attempted to bring Percy to his senses – firstly, with an abrupt dowsing of water and secondly, by the administration of ether.

At the age of twenty, John Polidori was remarkably young to be a medic and it is a testament to his prodigious intelligence that he was capable of gaining a medical degree from Edinburgh University when only nineteen. Although not a career path he had wholly embraced, the profession had, at least, led him to this gathering of creative minds, indulging in conversation that was more akin to his desired aims in life.

Polidori was from an Anglo-Italian family, resident in London's Soho. He was born in the September of 1795, just six years after his father, Gaetano, had arrived in the UK and moved into Broad Street, now Broadwick Street. The Italian émigré had married an English governess called Anna Maria Pierce and John was their second child. At the time of his birth, the couple were established at 38 Great Pulteney Street, a terraced town house in the heart of Soho.

In tracing John's early years, we made our way to his family home from Brewer Street and were soon presented with the four-storeyed smart frontage of the building which differs from its neighbours by wearing a classically inspired portico around its black front door. Today, the ground floor is plastered with cream render which offsets the exposed brickwork of the three floors above. The age of the building is given away by the characteristic metallic 'S' of a brace, between the uppermost storeys, designed to hold back the years.

At eye level is a circular, green City of Westminster plaque that records Polidori's authorship of *The Vampyre* . The date of its appearance is a much-belated 1998 and was the result of a small campaign by a few die-hard aficionados. Although the basic shape of the property cannot have changed since the eighteenth century, the surrounding built environment has radically altered. In terms of populace, the Soho of

1789 was perhaps the beginning of the Soho we know today, an eclectic mix of tradespeople, artists, writers, bon viveurs and ne'er do wells.

It was the ideal entry-point into English society for many immigrants, as seen in the street names; for example, Greek Street, D'Arblay Street and Dufours Place. Among the most numerous incomers were the aforementioned Greeks, Italians – much like Gaetano Polidori – and, on a greater scale, Protestant Huguenots escaping persecution in pre-revolutionary France. So large was the influx that Soho became London's French Quarter.

John's father lived in a relatively affluent part of the area but there were slum conditions in places like St Giles that were every bit as bad as the horrors to come in the Victorian era, evidenced by the rapid spread of cholera in the middle of the nineteenth century. Gaetano would have mixed with his fellow émigrés from Italy and a rich stew of French tailors, Greek merchants and people in search of the burgeoning enter-tainment industry. Adding to the piquancy was the inevitable underbelly of opportunists and chancers who fed the area's reputation for crime and prostitution.

At this point, given the influence it was to have on events in John's life, it is important to delve a little deeper into his father's backstory. Gaetano Polidori had been employed as a Secretary to the aristocratic author, Count Vittorio Alfieri, who was known for his plethora of tragedies and   comedies. Gaetano had given up studying law at Pisa to take this   position owing to his desire for a career in the world of letters. In a move mirroring his son's attachment to Byron, Polidori Senior dropped everything to follow Alfieri from Italy to France. He helped the author in the compilation of his works and in communica-tions with publishers.

As John would also find to his cost, the role of underling to a famous man came at a price, especially if the man in question had less than an even temperament. Alfieri was a notorious depressive and had previ-ously attempted suicide. Amongst Gaetano's writings there are references and anecdotes that refer to the Count; in particular, there is one interesting story that reveals much about both men.

During a time that saw his employer recuperating his health, Gaetano was invited to spend the evenings with Alfieri and his mistress, the Countess of Albany, widow of Bonnie Prince Charlie. It seems that the Countess had taken a shine to Polidori's well-rounded thighs and, rather indecorously, remarked upon their difference to those of the author whose curt response was, "'stuff and nonsense'". The incident was not laughed off by Gaetano who found the comment coarse and unfitting for a woman of her status, although he would not have dared to voice his opinions. The upshot of this event was a summary banishment from such intimate evenings by the fireside. It must have smarted to no longer be regarded as part of the inner circle.

This small episode would have also piqued Alfieri's sense of himself as a lothario and lover, a man capable of duelling with a cuckolded husband and striking the pose of a Don Juan. In 1788, the Count moved to Paris drawn by both the Countess of Albany and his fascination with the politics of the era. Gaetano was struck dumb by the brutality he and Alfieri witnessed as they toured the revolutionary streets of the city. Far from feeling his employer's joy at the destruction of the Bastille and the carnage that ensued, Polidori felt it was time to leave and head for London.

If one were to substitute the name John for Gaetano and the name Lord Byron for Count Alfieri, there would be little to amend in the unfolding of John's story, which has an uncanny symmetry with that of his father. As we will subsequently discover, the ambitious doctor refused to heed the words of warning his father issued with a heartfelt severity born of experience and hindsight.

Gaetano set himself up in England as a teacher of Italian and a translator, notably rendering Milton into his native tongue. He ensured that his first two children had a fluent grasp of Italian and English, also giving John the opportunity to become more than proficient in French. The young Polidori started his education at a Catholic school in Somers Town. The area is traditionally associated with a triangular patch of London between the roads of Hampstead, Pancras and Euston.

Many from France were drawn to the district in order to evade the worst excesses of the French Revolution. Interestingly, it was also home to the feminist writer Mary Wollstonecraft and her husband William Godwin, the theorist and novelist. They lived in a zone known as The Polygon which, as we discovered, is now home to a rather mundane block of council flats whose one link to this past is a plaque commemorating Mary's residence and her authorship of A *Vindication of the Rights of Woman*.

Sadly, Mary Wollstonecraft was to die giving birth to her second child, also named Mary, whose path would later cross with Polidori's on the shores of Lake Geneva, where she would create her most famous novel, *Frankenstein*. Given their similar ages, and despite the Godwin family's move to Skinner Street, it is fun to speculate whether John and Mary ever unwittingly brushed shoulders in the Somers Town of their youth.

The seven-year old John was not to remain at the Somers Town school for any length of time. Gaetano had far grander ideas and was wary of the nefarious influences such a transient population was having on his young son. A period of private tutoring revealed Polidori's prodigious scholarly ability and this may have had a bearing on the family's decision to send the boy to Yorkshire where he boarded at the newly-opened Ampleforth College, site of a Benedictine Abbey. He must have felt that he had been ripped from the body of his family, leaving behind his sisters, Maria, Frances and Charlotte.

The school had been established by monks from the Abbey and initially had around seventy students. It gradually expanded and is still, to this day, an independent educational institution of repute. The list of alumni is littered with famous names from the worlds of religion, business, medicine and culture, including Cardinal Basil Hume, Michael Ancram – former Deputy Leader of the Conservative Party, the actor Rupert Everett and Julian Fellowes, the writer of Downton Abbey. The location is a very rural one and would have been a complete culture shock to a boy more used to the frenetic environs of Soho.

As can be imagined, the intended purpose of such an establishment at the time of Polidori's attendance was to prepare its pupils for the priesthood, albeit not exclusively, as is evidenced by John's own career path. However, the isolated ecclesiastical atmosphere must have seeped into his consciousness as, at one point, he wrote home to his father about his inclination towards a priestly vocation, "for I have thought for a great while that it was my calling". Ever the sage yet stern parent, Gaetano would not hear of it, nor would he encourage a suggestion from his wife's brother that a military career be considered. With regard to the latter proposal, the young Polidori was mightily relieved.

There are hints in John's subsequent writing of moments during his time at Ampleforth when his sensitive nature was easily damaged by the vocal and physical barbs of more robust students. His 1818 text *An Essay Upon The Source of Positive Pleasure* contains this passage of rose-tinted prose, punctured by bitter recall:

> The boy, educated in a town, will remember, in his old age, the lime-shaded play-ground, and the hoary antique church. He will paint in more vivid colours than the painter's pallet will afford, the mellowing tints of eve, which threw a rosy glow upon the steeple's top . . . He does not bring to his remembrance, how the plain before the school often received him, harassed by the pedantic rule of his pedagogue, to give him up to the more tormenting tyranny of an infant Hercules.

In terms of learning, John excelled, taking full advantage of the curriculum offered which naturally focussed on the comprehension and composition of Latin. The biblical languages of Greek and Hebrew also featured and he had an excellent natural backdrop to enhance his studies of geography. As notions of a religious career faded, exchanges with his father concentrated on the boy's next steps.

A clue to the decision taken can be found in Gaetano's publishing of a book in verse-form called *Osteologia*. The text was a study of human bone structure and was written by John's grandfather, Agostino Ansano Polidori, who had died in 1778. The man in question had been a surgeon and a well-respected medical man. In light of a family history in the discipline, Gaetano decided that the best possible course for his son was a career as a doctor. Therefore, on leaving Ampleforth, it was to Edinburgh University that he went to take up a degree in medicine.

The university had a Europe-wide reputation for its medical studies but, as one might expect, the experience of an early nineteenth-century student would have been very different to that of a modern day would-be doctor. In 1811, Polidori was given a choice of subjects; with there being no set curriculum to follow, he plumped for a wide-ranging selection throughout his degree including anatomy, medicine, chemistry, botany and *Materia Medica*. Fees were not paid to the university but directly to the lecturers whose classes he attended. To say these men were an eccentric bunch is an understatement.

Firstly, there was James Gregory who took up the Chair of Medicine in 1790 and who was censured for being too free with the college's private correspondence, losing his fellowship in the process. James was the son of John, the quirky inventor of Gregory's Powder – a combination of rhubarb, magnesia and ginger that was used to quell a queasy stomach right up until the First World War. In fact, the family, seemingly consisting of a plethora of James' and Johns', appears to have had something of a fiefdom at the heart of the medical school. This did not, however, stop them from conflicting with other members of the faculty. A colleague, James Hamilton, produced *A Guide for Gentlemen Studying Medicine at the University of Edinburgh*, a tome that Polidori would undoubtedly have seen. It seems that the book created a *cause célèbre* when it denigrated some of the professors.

Gregory Junior was so incensed, having commissioned the text, that he confronted Hamilton with the fall force of his indignation. The unrepentant Hamilton then felt the physical force of the professor's cane. This unseemly debacle led to a law suit which saw Gregory pay £100 in damages, not an inconsiderable sum at the time. He even went as far as to say that he would happily have paid double to have another go.

Hamilton was a notorious litigant and would find opportunities to sue at the drop of a hat. Not so, the far more convivial Andrew Duncan, one of the first men to campaign for a public lunatic asylum which was finally opened during Polidori's time as a student in 1813. In addition to his good works, Duncan was a very sociable man who started societies such as the Harveian and Aesculapian; the latter being named after the Greek God of Medicine, and the former in celebration of the discovery of blood circulation with the added aim of forming kindly relationships amongst those in the medical profession. It is easy to see how he gained his reputation for being a benign and intelligent man.

As was the way of things in Edinburgh, another doctor, James Home succeeded his father, Francis, in the Chair of *Materia Medica*, a subject we know Polidori studied. In essence, this topic concerns the collected knowledge regarding the therapeutic properties of any substance used for healing. Homes' lectures were well-attended and histories of the university suggest that his favoured 8 a.m. start was packed with eager participants, although this was a phenomenon that declined when he was transferred to the Chair of Physic eight years after John had qualified.

A further example of nepotistic appointment can be detected in the story of the Monros. Alexander Monro the Second petitioned for his son to be appointed his successor to the Chair of Anatomy. After some gentle discussion, Alexander Monro the Third took up joint Chairmanship with his father, assuming sole possession after his death. This conniving manoeuvre had already taken place higher up the family tree between Alexander the First and his son.

Polidori drew the short straw in that Monro the Third was such a dreadful teacher he simply fell to reiterating his grandfather's notes. This gem of complaint comes from a contemporary student's letter: "He used to read his grandfather's lectures written about a century before; and even the shower of peas with which the expectant students greeted his annual reference, 'When I was a student in Leyden in 1719,' failed to induce him to alter the dates." Monro's lectures were so boring that they even put Charles Darwin off the subject of anatomy as he clearly states in his autobiography, noting that the doctor "made his lectures on human anatomy as dull as he was himself, and the subject disgusted me".

Into this fevered atmosphere of litigation, dynastic machination, academic lottery and the early flickerings of the Age of Science, entered the fresh-faced young Anglo-Italian. He took lodgings in Buccleuch Place, now as then, a popular area for student accommodation. Today, one side of the cobbled road maintains its characteristic nineteenth-century Edinburgh tenements, whilst the other has given way to the glass and concrete of the 1970s.

Incredibly, Polidori was just sixteen years old and mixing with students from the Americas and Europe. It seems he was somewhat withdrawn and preferred the company of continental Europeans rather than the Scottish students who thought him "a pedant", as he pointed out in one letter home to his father. From the outset, he felt antagonistic towards this choice of career foisted upon him and found no stimulating debate or burning interest in the lectures he attended, especially those of the aforementioned droning Monro. It seems most likely that he would have paid for additional anatomical tuition in order to gain a grasp of the subject that was not afforded him by Alexander the Third.

Working under Monro was the anatomist Andrew Fyfe who would have undertaken demonstrations in the dissecting theatre. He was also thought to be a mediocre lecturer but possessed good practical skills he could pass on to his students. The difficulty in performing these post-mortem operations was the lack of useable cadavers, as the law forbade the use of any bodies except those of prisoners, suicide victims and orphans. Unsurprisingly, opportunity and poverty combined to create the trade in grave-robbing and certain professors would ask no questions. One such was Polidori's fellow student, Robert Knox, who would go on to become an acclaimed anatomist and Fellow of the Royal Society of Edinburgh.

He is chiefly remembered, however, for his involvement in the case of Burke and Hare. The gruesome events took place thirteen years after John had graduated. The infamous duo made the obvious if ghoulish leap from grave-robbing, where the quality of the corpse could not be guaranteed, to the murder of vulnerable victims. The whole series of macabre events was triggered by the natural death of a lodger in Hare's guesthouse, witnessed by fellow lodger, Burke. Hare sold the cadaver to Knox's anatomy school and realized there was money to be made. When an argument broke out with another guest over rent, the pair smothered him to death and duly delivered the body to the anatomist.

However, as time went on, they became careless over their choice of victims and made the mistake of selecting people who, although poor and susceptible, were, nonetheless, well-known in the community. Sudden disappearances became suspicious and their ultimate undoing was the arrival on the dissecting table of a prostitute familiar to many students during drunken nights of revelry. She had previously been seen in the company of Burke and Hare.

The law enforcers paid a visit to Hare's boarding house and made the ghastly discovery of a young woman's body stuffed inside a mattress. With both facing the noose, Hare made the decision to confess all, turning King's evidence against Burke who was unceremoniously hung. The toxicologist and physician, Robert Christison, interviewed Robert Knox, who claimed that the nefarious duo had simply watched lodging houses and bought corpses before they could be buried. Luckily for Knox, he escaped any stain in the courts because Burke had exonerated him. The journalists of the day, however, were not so sure and this rhyme could be heard in the streets of Edinburgh: "Up the close and doon the stair, / But and ben' wi' Burke and Hare. / Burke's the butcher, Hare's the thief, / Knox the boy that buys the beef."

Although the anatomists of Polidori's day were happy to receive corpses, they never stooped to these depths. Despite the lectures he attended on the body, it was the mind that was of greater interest to our young student. He took the rather unorthodox decision to make somnambulism the subject of his thesis. The paper had to be presented in Latin, which was no problem for a clerically educated Catholic like Polidori. The translated title of his thesis was the rather wordy: *A Medical Inaugural Dissertation which deals with the disease called Oneirodynia, for the degree of Medical Doctor Edinburgh 1815.*

Polidori quoted a Dr Cullen in his attempt to clarify sleepwalking: "Cullen divides the disease into two types: one, as activity and the impulse towards walking and various movements, and the second, the patient's being burdened by the sensation that the chest is being compressed by a dead weight." The second statement is a significant one and calls to mind the 1781 painting by Henry Fuseli, the expatriate Swiss artist who painted *The Nightmare*. Apart from his painting of Mary Wollstonecraft, Mary Shelley's mother, *The Nightmare* is Fuseli's most well-known work. A recumbent woman, stretched out on a bed, eyes closed and in the throes of a bad dream, has the very manifestation of her delusion, an incubus, perched malevolently on her chest, his intentions clearly not honourable.

The tableau is gazed upon by the curious addition of a wide-eyed horse, associated in folklore with the topic of nightmares, specifically of the German variety that has lone-sleeping men being visited by horses and hags, whilst solitary women engage in sex with the devil. From the supine position of the female protagonist in Fuseli's picture, and the almost ecstatic expression on her face, it is unsurprising that the painting was condemned by subsequent Victorian moralists as too sexually overt.

The demonic nature and Gothic imagery of the original were further enhanced in the engraved version of the painting by the addition of these lines from Erasmus Darwin: "So on his Nightmare through the evening fog / Flits the squab Fiend o'er fen, and lake, and bog; / Seeks some love-wilder'd maid with sleep oppress'd, / Alights, and grinning sits upon her breast." Given the popularity of Fuseli's work, it is very difficult to imagine that Polidori would not have had this visual representation of the unconscious flitting through his thoughts as he turned his mind to the medical causes of the condition.

He cites a number of predisposing circumstances that may lead to Darwin's "sleep oppress'd" nights which include alcohol, foodstuffs, lying supine and the usage of opium, all of which he would later encounter in Byron's circle. Luckily, John was able to call on a case study written up by his uncle, Dr Aloysius Eustace Polidori. Aloysius witnessed a boy rise from a brief sleep, gesticulating and babbling words. When interrupted, the boy began to throw punches at a servant, seemingly hysterical and suffering from spasms. John interpreted this as "a serious overstimulation of the brain and nervous system", but also admitted that "the nature of this affliction of the brain is beyond our current knowledge".

He suggested two procedures in the treatment of somnambulism – firstly to stop the paroxysms and secondly to dispel the underlying symptoms. He recommended the removal of predisposing factors such as drink and mental overstimulation, together with the administering of a tonic he called Portuguese bark which we know today as quinine.

John successfully defended his thesis in front of the doctors Hope, Gregory, Horne and the infamous Monro. On the back of his original paper, he scribbled the following description:

> After my examination, having been put out of the room, Dr Hope came to me and said that I had not only passed but passed with the utmost satisfaction to all the Professors and upon my going out, Dr Monro complemented me upon my extraordinary clear head. Next morning I called upon Dr Gregory about my thesis, who told me that in my case there was no fear of rejection in my ulterior trial so that my thesis might be delivered to the printers, which I did accordingly . . . And on 1st of August, I was examined upon my thesis by Dr Gregory who after prefacing that it was quam maxima in gennitate ad quam – attached my dissertation of Oneirodynia which I however supported. On that day I received the award for all my troubles and was, by the imposition of the velvet cap, raised to the Degree of Doctor of Medicine.

James Gregory's *"quam maxima"* indicates the highest level of attainment and, clearly, Polidori was an intellect to be reckoned with, particularly when considering he had graduated at the age of nineteen, just one month short of his twentieth birthday, and that he had no real interest in medicine. Despite this startling achievement, during the course of his degree he realized he needed extra time to cram his studies having let his attention wane. In fact, his university years saw him begin to cultivate his real passion for literature, an interest that led him to Norwich in the autumn of his graduation.

Poetry and drama, in particular, were his two passions, fed by the *Edinburgh Review* – the respected magazine that had been founded in 1802 and whose circulation figures rose to peak levels during John's time in the city. It was the same magazine that tore into Byron's early poetry, prompting the satirical repost in verse that was the 1809 poem 'English Bards and Scotch Reviewers'. Here we have Byron venting his spleen and honing his poetic craft: "Say! Will not Caledonia's annals yield / The glorious record of some nobler field, / Than the wild foray of a plundering clan, / Whose proudest deeds disgrace the name of man?"

Polidori's satisfied parents were able to smile benignly on these poetical fixations as they now had a qualified doctor for a son, albeit one
who was more interested in the dramas he attempted to write at university, notably *Count Orlando*, than he was in blood-letting a patient
suffering from *Porphyria cutanea tarda*. With this attitude firmly
entrenched, John left his family home in Soho to head for Norwich, a
destination that he had already visited towards the end of his studies.
The attraction was the circle of like-minded souls created by William
Taylor, a proponent of German Romantic literature and a contributor
to the *Monthly Review*.

Taylor liked to surround himself with a group of aspirant young men
with literary and philosophical inclinations. His privileged background as a merchant's son, based in Surrey Street, afforded him the
luxury of travel and a continental finish to his well-rounded education.
He was the conduit that introduced the best of German literature from
the period to a hitherto ignorant British populace and was also a
founder member of the Norwich Revolutionary Society, a position that
occasionally saw him confront the authorities. Facing a seemingly
imminent threat of arrest, the society was disbanded in 1794 and
Taylor took up less political pursuits.

Among the many who came to William's literary gatherings were
Robert Southey, John Warden Robberds and George Borrow. Borrow,
the famous polyglot and author of *The Bible in Spain*, was not quite a
contemporary of Polidori, given he would have been only twelve years
of age when John visited in 1815. Nevertheless, Borrow has left for
posterity a fascinating portrait of Taylor in his quasi-fictional autobiographical account, *Lavengro,* a portrait they would have both
recognized. The curious title of the book is Romany for 'word-master'
and refers to the gypsy community's name for the author.

Written in the early 1840s, the text harks back to the years Borrow
spent debating with Taylor and contains this vivid image:

> The forehead of the elder individual was high, and perhaps
> appeared more so than it really was, from the hair being carefully
> brushed back, as if for the purpose of displaying to the best advan-
> tage that part of the cranium; his eyes were large and full, and of

a light brown, and might have been called heavy and dull, had they not been occasionally lighted up by a sudden gleam – not so brilliant however as that which at every inhalation shone from the bowl of the long clay pipe which he was smoking . . .

The younger man in the scenario created above, tells the veiled version of Taylor that he does not want to take up smoking, bringing the repost that smoking is the path to becoming a good German. "It is good to be a German; the Germans are the most philosophic people in the world, and the greatest smokers . . . " is the elder's summation of the short exchange. We are clearly in the presence of a worldly man with continental leanings; a man who translated Goethe's *Iphigenie on Taurus* and brought him to the attention of a wider public. The Anglo-German cultural exchange moved in both directions – Goethe was a fervent admirer of Byron.

Polidori flourished in Taylor's company and that of the group now formally known as the Speculative Society. The removal of his intellectual straightjacket allowed him to blossom and he proffered his opinions without any more fear of being called a pedant. The aforementioned Robberds captures the atmosphere well in his book about Taylor: "Young men who evinced any taste for literature were urged forward and assisted in their pursuits . . . His time, his advice, his books, his table, and not infrequently his purse also, were most liberally at their service."

Polidori was clearly not just a hanger-on. Taylor even anticipates his visit in a letter to the renowned Southey, claiming that our half-Italian doctor had "written two tragedies in that language". Sadly, no trace remains of these works and it is even conceivable that William was confusing Polidori's ancestral identity with the English language dramas penned at university.

It was not only his intellect that attracted those around him, but also his Mediterranean looks, combined with pale Anglo-Saxon skin. A local portrait painter sketched him as the God, Apollo, complete with laurels and an accompanying annotation that praises his poetic gifts before his medical profession. Perhaps the best description of Polidori at this time comes from no less a figure than Harriet Martineau, the essayist, novelist and proto-feminist descended from French Huguenots.

Ahead of her time, she was able to make a living from writing alone and was so recognized that she was invited to attend Queen Victoria's coronation. In her early teens, at the time of Polidori's visit, she remembered him in her autobiography written many years later, although some of these references undoubtedly refer to his subsequent visits:

> It was poor Polidori, well-known afterwards as Lord Byron's physician, as the author of *The Vampyre* – When we knew him, he was a handsome, harum-scarum young man, taken up by William Taylor as William Taylor did take up harum-scarum young men . . . he was an avowed admirer of our elder sister (who however escaped fancy-free;) and he was forever at our house. We younger ones romanced amazingly about him, – drew his remarkable profile on the backs of all our letters , dreamed of him, listened to all his marvelous stories . . .

Norwich gave Polidori the opportunity to temporarily release the captive Romantic that he truly wanted to be. He clearly demonstrated a youthful vigour, perhaps pronouncing on subjects about which he had little knowledge but was overly-enthusiastic to investigate further. We have a vision of him at this juncture as a young man still at odds with himself, partially unaware of his impact on the opposite sex, and voracious in his attempts to tackle every conceivable philosophical subject without stopping to distil the essence of the topic.

Yet what was Polidori to do now? John's ideal would have been employment as a physician in Norwich where he could maintain contacts with his literary friends and stay close to the King Street residence of William Taylor. Alas for the would-be medic, Harriet's father, Dr Martineau, and a certain Dr Rigby had the medical field stitched up. Other options were considered including working as a physician under the British East India Company in the subcontinent or relocating to Italy. Both were discarded as too precarious and without backing. A confused Polidori confided his desperation to his sister, Frances, and was becoming increasingly resigned to a middling doctor's position in suburban London.

This path, however, had a hurdle that only time could overcome. Nobody at Edinburgh bothered to inform the young student that London had its own specific rules regarding the right to practise; not only did John have to pass the city's own medical examinations, he also had to wait until he was twenty-six to be allowed to set himself up as a doctor. There was no question of adopting some clandestine approach to circumvent these rules as the long arm of the law would have swiftly intervened. Polidori was facing the prospect of sitting on his hands for six years or looking elsewhere.

To keep himself occupied, he sought solace in writing and produced an essay on capital punishment entitled 'On the Punishment of Death', later published in *The Pamphleteer*. He set out an argument against the death penalty which is a forceful precursor to the ideas that finally saw Britain dispense with hanging over a century later:

> If it is our wish to make vice shrink and virtue flourish, let us show we pay some attention to honesty; let us not punish various degrees of vice with equal infliction, let us appreciate what little virtue there is even in the wretch amenable to our laws.
>
> Has not the experience of ages shown us the insufficiency of capital punishments? Does not Asia, Europe, Africa, American, every people, every nation, nay every village of this sublunary world, demonstrate the insufficiency of this punishment?

At the age of twenty, Polidori was openly wearing his Romantic and liberal credentials but solid employment eluded him. Into the metaphorical and literal gloom of Soho's Pulteney Street stepped Robert Gooch, an old boy of Edinburgh and newly acquired friend of John's. Gooch worked under the patronage of Sir William Knighton, physician to the Prince Regent, and came to Polidori with the news that Knighton was on the look-out for a physician to accompany Lord Byron abroad and had seemingly recommended him.

A letter exists from Byron's half-sister, Augusta, to the poet's friend, Francis Hodgson, which suggests that the aristocrat had been talking to Knighton about Polidori. In his biography, *Polidori!*, Franklin Bishop proposes that Sir William had met John at Edinburgh and had been impressed by him. We have not been able to find evidence of this meeting but, whether by word of mouth or in person, it is clear that Knighton felt sufficiently confident in his recommendation.

At this stage in his life, Lord Byron or George Gordon the 6th Baron Byron, was in the middle of a crisis. The celebrity poet who had become famous, almost overnight, thanks to the success of his work, *Childe Harold*, was now in the midst of agonizing marital turmoil of his own making. Having lived through a series of tempestuous relationships with society belles, more often than not married, Byron, who would be christened "mad, bad and dangerous to know" by former lover, Lady Caroline Lamb, had been persuaded to take a wife. The unfortunate lady in question was Annabella Milbanke.

Annabella was not blind to his reputation and, indeed, turned down an initial invite to meet. On the surface, she was not Byron's usual type, displaying a level-headed intellect that ran contrary to his erratic passions. Perhaps it was a case of opposite characters attracting to balance out each other's distinct personalities. For Byron, Annabella represented a steadying tiller and she believed herself capable of steering him to less tortuous waters.

Childe Harold and subsequent poems, such as *The Corsair*, feature the quintessential Byronic hero, the restless, self-sabotaging soul at odds with society. We will certainly not be the first or last to point out biographical similarities between the author and his Childe, although Byron always maintained there were none, apart from "trivial particulars". We suspect this was said with a sardonic smirk. Certainly during the poet's marriage, he lived up to the more restless and reckless aspects of his characters' lives. Byron did not take long to find Annabella irritating and, as Peter Quennell in his biography, *Byron: The Years of Fame*, points out, the aristocrat even awoke on his wedding night with the cry "'Good God, I am surely in Hell!'"

Byron seemed in the midst of a persecution complex, convinced he would be damned and punished. These notions led to hints of wrongdoing and ravings that truly frightened Annabella. After his honeymoon or as the poet retitled it, his "treacle moon" at Halnaby Hall, the couple initially stayed with the Milbankes in Seaham on the Durham coast, which bizarrely, given his aversion to the place, has a street named Lord Byron's Walk. From there, they went to visit Byron's half-sister, Augusta, in Six Mile Bottom near Newmarket. The aristocrat was reluctant to take his wife, a clue to the triangle at the core of his disintegrating marriage.

Augusta was always uppermost in Byron's affections which were not simply brotherly. There is much substance to the inferences of incest that have followed the poet in life and death. At the time of a previous stay with his half-sister, when her husband was absent, he admitted in a letter to Thomas Moore of "a new and serious scrape" with an unspecified lover. It is also thought that he spilled his heart to his confidante, Lady Melbourne, who warned him of the consequences — consequences that were now coming home to roost as Annabella shared a house with Augusta.

Annabella could never hope to match Augusta's easy way with Byron and their shared history of an absent and unreliable father. The sexual transgression piqued Byron's sense of dangerous rule-breaking yet, in her company, he found his home. Annabella was left with the bitter dregs of his humour.

Eventually, the unhappily married couple moved to 13 Piccadilly Terrace near Hyde Park in London and Annabella gave birth to their only child christened with a name that must have been a knife through the mother's heart — Augusta Ada, later known as just Ada. By now, Annabella's parents had become acquainted with a list of their son-in-law's vices and there were many who wanted to fan the flames of scandal — not least the jilted Lady Caroline Lamb. To incest we can add the charge of sodomy, then illegal, and a taboo in polite society. Byron was fluid in his sexuality and had displayed homosexual feelings since his school days. The Grand Tour to Greece, Albania and Turkey in 1809 gave him free reign to experiment; seemingly, he also included a naïve and shocked Annabella in his nostalgic and unlawful desires.

Byron's tall poppy was about to be scythed to its roots by a scandal which had been whipped up gleefully by those who wanted to see him brought down. In the face of constant attack and a wife drip-fed with poisonous rumour, he saw no choice but to acquiesce to separation and exile. At this juncture, William Knighton's emissary, Gooch, arrives on Polidori's doorstep with the offer of employment. To a confused and directionless John, this must have seemed like manna from heaven with the added glamour of endless days spent discussing his beloved literature with a famous poet.

His father's reaction, however, was the polar opposite. Gaetano, having experienced life with the writer and aristocrat, Alfieri, knew the perils awaiting his son. Initially, John withdrew his acceptance but could not resist the allure of such an opportunity. Andrew McConnell Stott in his excellent *The Vampyre Family* quotes from a letter Gaetano wrote to his brother, Luigi, saying of his son "his youthful fancy so excited that, in that heat, he ran off to Lord Byron, and re-spun the broken thread, contrary to my advice". Polidori was now on the edge of a very complex web.

CHAPTER TWO

The Low Countries
Flemish Faces

The date was 22 April 1816. Byron was waiting at Piccadilly Terrace in the company of his friends, John Cam Hobhouse and Scrope Davies. A knock at the door is answered by one of his three servants, either the Swiss, Berger, employed for the forthcoming journey, the faithful Fletcher or the young page, Rushton. Standing on the threshold is a tall, dark and eager young man, his curls falling gently across a pale forehead. His high white shirt collar is supported by an elaborate neck-cloth projecting the dandified air of a Regency beau, further heightened by the sweep of a jet black coat drawn across his chest.

Polidori is beckoned inside where he comes face to face with his employer. Apart from Byron's long patrician nose and dimpled chin, any onlooker would have been struck by the similarity in their colouring and flamboyant dark curls. Indeed, Byron once remarked that when looking at his physician, it was like seeing his younger self in a mirror. In many ways, John's appearance would have been the aspiration for many and we can easily conjecture that prickles of jealousy were the motive for Byron's compliment.

If the aristocrat appeared pleased by his new "acquisition", then Polidori must have been quivering with trepidation and over-excitement. Byron's two friends were a little more circumspect and wary of the giddy young man before them. Many biographers have been swayed by Hobhouse's almost instantaneous dislike for Polidori. The poet's friend and confidante, Thomas Moore, gives this bitter description of the doctor: "His mind, accordingly, between ardour and weakness, was kept in a constant hectic of vanity . . . " Many decades later, Peter Quennell in *The Years of Fame*, assigns John notions of grandeur and

The Dijver,
Bruges,
S. Edwards

*The Ghent
Altarpiece by the van
Eyck Brothers in St
Bavo Cathedral in
Ghent,* Pierre
François De Noter,
1829,
Rijksmuseum

Antwerp Cathedral, Juulz Grand, Pixabay

Battlefield of Waterloo, H. Gérard (possibly), 1842, Rijksmuseum

ineptitude which seem to be inspired directly from the pen of Hobhouse.

Later to be the 1st Baron Broughton, John Cam Hobhouse had already accompanied Byron on his Grand Tour starting in 1809, and was the plodding foil to Byron's impetuosity. When George Gordon was taken by the muse, Hobhouse would be making scrupulous notes or writing in his journal. It was in this diary that he would later refer to Polidori in the following terms: "He is anything but an amiable man, and has a most unmeasured ambition, as well as inordinate vanity." Both of the above quotations shine a poor light on our doctor, but both come from intimate friends of the poet who would not contradict Byron's increasingly negative opinion of the physician or his own monstrous vanity.

For the time being, however, Byron was satisfied with the company of John as the household made preparations to leave. Nevertheless, Polidori would always be at a disadvantage owing to his lack of years and social status, despite being an intellectual equal. On the following day, the 23rd, Hobhouse, much to his dismay, was relegated to Scrope Davies' chaise with John, whilst Byron boarded his ludicrous copy of Napoleon's carriage which he had commissioned but neglected to pay for. It is telling that soon after the carriages had disappeared from Piccadilly, a more sinister convoy appeared carrying the bailiffs who entered the property and seized the remainder of Byron's possessions, including his library.

The plan was to head for Dover and embark for the continent as soon as possible. The party stayed at the Ship Hotel on the Custom House Quay looking out over what is now Granville Dock. The carriages would have pulled up outside the canopied frontage facing the English Channel. The anticipation of an early departure was dashed by the weather and so the group amused themselves on the following day with a walk along the cliffs and a visit to St Mary's Church.

The purpose of the visit was to pay homage to the grave of the then-famous writer, Charles Churchill. Churchill had been a poet and satirist, immortalized by the celebrated Hogarth. Hobhouse matter-of-factly picks up the story: "We asked the Sexton what Churchill was celebrated for. He said, 'He died before my time, though I have been here thirty-five year. I had not the burying of him'. However, being again asked, he said 'For his writings.' Byron lay down on his grave, and gave the man a crown to fresh-turf it." This dramatic gesture is typical of the man who had once drunk from a human skull converted to a wine goblet.

Polidori, who had been delighted to receive the offer of £500 from John Murray to document his time with the poet, was already hard at work on his diary which will be our guide to the travels that lie ahead. It is clear from the Dover entries that Byron's dramatic gesture and subsequent largesse had much more effect on our wannabe author, causing him to muse on the vagaries of fame:

> There were two authors; one, the most distinguished of his age; another, whose name is rapidly rising; (and a third, ambitious for literary distinction). What a lesson it was for them when, having asked the sexton if he knew why so many came to see this tomb, he said: 'I cannot tell; I had not the burying of him.'

The doctor is vain enough to include himself in brackets amongst such exalted company but does not display the "hectic of vanity" attributed to him by Thomas Moore, but rather a more subtle insight into the fleeting nature of literary fame. This was certainly true with regard to Churchill's reputation given that he is barely known today and, when we visited St Mary's, there was merely a plaque present – his tomb having fallen foul of the developers.

There are hints in this passage of John's desire to further his ambitions and it took him little time to show a manuscript of one of his plays to the assembled group that evening in the hotel. The initial reading, carried out in a mocking tone, was met with howls of laughter. The second, more conciliatory reading was listened to with attention but Polidori's feelings had already been hurt. We can hear the wounded pride in his words, "having delivered my play into their hands, I had to hear it laughed at".

In his first real meeting with true literary aristocracy, Polidori had been firmly put in his place. His biographer, Franklin Bishop, is convinced that the initial reading was done by a scornful Hobhouse and he cites

John Cam's journal as evidence: "Dr Polidori committed a strange sole-cism tonight, and had the naiveté to tell us of it. He was lectured by both – his attachment to reputation, and his three tragedies, is most singular and ridiculous. Byron says he shall have the reputation of having made a sober commonplace fellow quite mad."

So deep was Polidori's pain, he makes a very cryptic entry in his diary that bodes very ill for future proceedings. He says, "I afterwards went out, and did a very absurd thing, which I told; and found I had not only hurt myself but might possibly hurt others for whom I cared much more." Are these the dark hints of suicidal thoughts or the mere ramblings of disappointed youth?

Whatever the issues of the night before, daylight brought the much-awaited departure. From the boat, the party waved farewell to Hobhouse and Scrope Davies standing on the Dover dockside. Polidori writes of his last sight of England in less than sentimental terms: "The coast of Dover is very striking, though miserably barren-looking. The cliff is steep, though not such as Shakespeare paints. The castle – at a distance, which is the only way I viewed it – is miserable." The crossing was largely uneventful, although there are hints in John's account of the grief felt by the group, which must be attributable to the reason behind their flight to the continent.

Their boat docked in Ostend, then part of the Netherlands, at two o'clock in the morning. With typical sang-froid, Byron dashed off a letter to Hobhouse recounting the voyage.

> As a veteran I stomached the sea pretty well – till a damned "Merchant of Bruges" capsized his breakfast close by me – & made me sick by contagion: – but I soon got well – & we were landed at least ten hours sooner than expected – and our Inn (the "Cure imperial" as Fletcher calls it -) furnished us with beds & a "flagon of Rhenish" – which – by the blessing of Scrope's absence – the only blessing his absence could confer – was not indulged in to the extent of the "light wine" of our parting potations.

He follows this up with a request to Hobhouse, who would be joining the party later in the year once they had reached Geneva. The prompt in question is the bold and urgent appeal: "Don't forget the Cundums." Clearly, Byron was not planning a chaste retreat. One of the most oft-cited passages from John's diary refers to Byron's prophylactic-free exploits with the first serving-girl he encountered in Ostend. The quote "Lord Byron fell like a thunderbolt on the chambermaid" is, in itself, a fascinating window on the adventures Polidori's journal would go through before it saw the light of day in print.

Despite Murray's offer of money, John's writing never found favour with Byron's publisher, and the hand-written text was passed down to his sister, Charlotte Lydia Polidori, the quintessential maiden aunt. Something of a prude, she saw fit to edit out passages she considered improper, afterwards destroying the original manuscript. It is thanks to William Michael Rossetti, brother of the painter Dante Gabriel and John's nephew, that we have the quote in question. He had read the full text prior to Charlotte's prurient pruning. As with Byron's destroyed memoirs, we can only guess at the passages William could not remember and therefore was unable to reinstate.

These gaps in the diary have led authors to put their own spin on the missing content. Paul West, winner of the Literature Prize of the American Academy of Arts and Literature, took the journal and sexed up the content to provide a darkly Gothic, sordid account of the journey in his very readable *Lord Byron's Doctor*. In Ostend, he has Polidori graphically describing the encounter with the chambermaid:

> He roared at the very sight of this porcine-looking drab, as if he had seen none such in all his days, then fell to wrenching off her millinery with his hands and teeth until a goodly amount of flesh began to show, and yet she did not run away . . . He was upon her straightaway, with his parts released . . .

Chambermaids aside, the party was happy with the hotel which was actually called the Cour Imperiale and situated in the Rue de la Chapelle, now translated into Dutch as Kapellestraat – a long pedestrianized shopping street that cuts through the heart of the town. The Cour, an imposing cube with a porticoed entrance, no longer exists, but can be seen illustrated in old postcards as it was one of the few hotels recommended to foreign tourists. John Murray, who was also a publisher of guidebooks, issued the 1845 *A Handbook for Travellers on the Continent*. The guide mentions the hotel, but in the next breath damns all the town's inns, "none of them are very good" and advises against drinking the water, which was actually filtered rain.

The Ostend of 1816 was in the midst of a post-Napoleonic slump and was only remarkable for its fortifications. Travellers of the period noted the mute melancholy. In his *Observations* written in the same year, Henry Smithers has this to say, "the general inactivity, and silence that prevail, exhibit a character of departed magnificence". It was the development of the harbour and railway that reinvigorated the area and the modern mind associates the town with its ferry port.

It was the first time on his route to Italy that Polidori was able to seek out bookshops, but it certainly would not be his last. The stores of Ostend, however, had a surprise waiting – "books in every bookseller's window of the most obscene nature" – perhaps they had been used to catering for a standing garrison and its troops starved of female company.

Our flustered doctor entered one establishment and asked for something in his accomplished French. He was met with stony silence and shrugs of incomprehension, which prompted him to try out his rudimentary German. Probably mistaking this for execrably pronounced Dutch, the shop assistants burst out laughing. Self-consciously laughing along, he added insult to his own injury by knocking a quarto from one of the shelves which fell onto a young lady's head. He had been mesmerized by her eyes and was so embarrassed, he bought two unwanted books by way of recompense. He neglects to tell us if they were of a salacious nature.

Byron was more positive towards Ostend, and felt it compared favourably to provincial towns he had seen in Portugal and Spain. John even saw the renowned fortifications as "miserable" and comments on the "bigoted religionists and wild republicans", who had besieged them in their thousands. He was not sorry to be moving on when Byron intimated he was keen to head for Ghent by way of Bruges – the neighbour Ostend looked to for its fresh water when it was not collecting the rain in buckets. Bruges is still famed for its watery habitat, and like so many towns with fluvial arteries, it has inevitably been compared with Venice.

Bruges has an undeniable charm but, as we discovered whilst sitting in a café overlooking the Dijver canal behind the Stadhuis, it has one other thing in common with Venice, a plethora of eager tourists. We sat listening to one unfortunate Spaniard ordering a simple beer, only to be confronted with Bruges' most famous export, a beer menu with a bewildering array of choices. The amused waiter told him that Belgium was home to more than 1000 different brews. Spoilt for choice and panicking, he opted for a gin and tonic.

Having done our research, we sipped the local beer of choice, Brugge Zot, looking towards the gentle waters that masked the inundating mass of humanity behind us. In doing so, it was still possible to appreciate the town witnessed by Byron and his doctor. Their Bruges was ostensibly the same, yet a very different place. Tourism has done much to revitalize what was a settlement in decline and suffering from the kind of stagnation that also afflicted Ostend. Georges Rodenbach's *Bruges-La-Morte* is the finest evocation of a dying Bruges in the nineteenth century. The Belgian writer, Rodenbach, became associated with the town to such an extent that, to the French, he was its very personification.

The book's central character, Hugues Viane, a desperately grieving widower, is the mirror to the death he sees in the deserted streets and lifeless houses lining the mist-shrouded canals. This passage captures the sadness in his surroundings and his heart:

> he created an invisible telepathy between his soul and the inconsolable towers of Bruges.
>   That's why he had chosen Bruges, Bruges where the sea had retreated in the same way as his own happiness. This was a further example of the phenomenon of resemblance he had already seen, and his thoughts would be in synergy with the "greatest of the Grey Towns".

It is the water and its reflection under northern skies that gives the aura of despondency that clearly spoke to Rodenbach's sense of a depressed

Bruges. Musing on these thoughts and in need of some colour, we made our way to the Groeningemuseum, housing an impressive art collection and sandwiched between the Dijver and the Arentshuis Museum. There we were treated to the sumptuous brocaded blue and divine red of the clothing worn by Canon van der Paele and the Madonna in Jan van Eyck's masterwork, along with the Italianate *Last Judgement* painted by a Michelangelo-inspired Pieter Pourbus. Our meandering through gallery rooms, though, brought us face to face with an unexpected death.

Little did we know that, at the beginning of our journey, we would encounter Byron at the end of his. Taking up the space of an entire wall and unaccompanied by other works, was *Lord Byron on His Deathbed* painted by Joseph Denis Odevaere in 1826, two years after the poet's death and a mere ten years after Byron and his doctor had walked these very streets.

Odevaere is liberal with classical allusion, from the laurel leaves crowning Byron's ashen brow to the poet's lyre loosely cradled under his wilting arm. In the distance, through an open window, we can make out an Olympian mountain behind the ruins of a temple, and above Byron's chaise is a draped golden statue bearing the Greek word *'Eleftheria'* meaning 'freedom'. Odevaere has sensitively positioned the sheet covering Byron, in such a manner that his misshapen foot remains hidden from view, hiding any hint of imperfection.

This semi-deification of a hero is obviously an idealistic portrayal of the man who did, indeed, put his weight behind the fight for Greek independence from the Turks. However, his death was not the glorious ending of a warrior-poet but a rather sad demise in the Missolonghi swamps addled with fever and weakened by years of hedonism. His brow would not have been so smooth and his torso so chiselled. This is myth-making in its most heightened form and a symbolistic view of Byron that Polidori was only just beginning to translate into reality. For now, we will respectfully leave the proto-Greek God to his eternal tragedy.

Nearly a century separated Rodenbach from Polidori, but the torpor of Bruges would have been the same. Our doctor had no time to visit galleries, but his diary reflects the simple joy of being "abroad". He, like many today, found the town at its most seductive as night settled on the waters, "twilight softened all the beauty, and I do not know how to describe the feeling of pleasure we felt in going through its long roof-fretted streets". He is referring to the characteristic stepped-gables on Belgium and Dutch canal-side houses, their geometric pattern lending a playful angularity to the town's silhouettes.

On leaving Bruges, Polidori turned to a theme he would mention again and again in his diary, namely the female Flemish face. Although he found the women "generally pretty", something he would later contradict, he thought the quintessential face had "no divinity". The kind of divinity he was seeking, the secular mixed with the religious, is a staple of the art he was yet to admire in depth. Ghent would change all that.

Firstly, however, there was the minor matter of navigating the scattered carriage paths to the town. John was awoken by Byron with the words, "'They have lost their way'". This seemingly innocuous comment hid a deeper problem. Not for them the fifty-minute drive down the motorway guided by a sat nav that took us from Bruges to Ghent. Their fear of finding themselves lost was rooted in the legends of the *Bokkenrijders*, originally demons mounted on satanic flying goats who swept the skies, cleverly co-opted by demons of a different sort – roving brigands in search of wealthy travellers and peaceful, undefended settlements.

It was now a wide-awake Polidori who was spooked by the empty house that he had approached, hoping to find a welcoming haven. Sufficiently worried to arm himself with a pistol, he rapped on the door repeatedly; other nearby houses were similarly silent. Had the *Bokkenrijders* already visited? The servants produced sabres and eventually the party managed to rouse a sleepy householder who mumbled the correct direction of travel. Remarkably, the postilion who had scarpered at the thought of a satanic visit, ignored the advice given and set the carriage on a route back to Bruges. Consequently, Byron and Polidori did not reach Ghent until the ungodly hour of 3 a.m.

After bribing the gatekeeper, they were admitted to the city centre and headed for the Hotel des Pays Bas in what was then called the Place d'Armes but is now known as the Kouter and the traditional home of major celebrations. Even at the beginning of the nineteenth century, the square had none of the quaint folksy charm of Bruges but rather proclaimed the industrial power of the merchant classes in a developing city. The Pays Bas, no longer a hotel, is part of the Ing Bank chain, but maintains its classical facade.

The heart of medieval Ghent is further to the north and centred on St Baafskathedraal and the Niklaaskerk. John was most taken with the cathedral's decoration, comparing it favourably with anything to be found in Britain, "after having been accustomed to the tinselly ornaments of our Catholic chapels, and the complete want of any in the Scotch and English churches, we were much pleased with the Cathedral's inside dress". Significantly, Polidori has slipped into using "we", thereby associating his own opinions with those of his illustrious travelling companion. Time and experience would erase this happy use of the first person plural, extinguishing the notion that Polidori belonged to Byron's inner circle.

St Bavo's, as it is known in English, is home to *The Ghent Altarpiece* by Hubert and Jan van Eyck which only used to be opened on feast days. The monumental panels, in two layers, contain many images with Christ, Mary and John the Baptist at the centre. Today, the artwork is sectioned off from the main body of the cathedral and requires a separate ticket. Curiously, Polidori makes no specific mention of this masterwork, choosing instead to focus on the macabre crypt, specifically the carved draperies on a tomb relief. Such an omission would have been even more puzzling at the time, given the panels of the artwork had only just been returned having been stolen by Napoleonic troops.

The party decided to ascend the steps to the top of the steeple, carefully counting each of the 450 steps that John makes sure we appreciate by reiterating their number. As they caught their breath, he took this mental picture of a low-country panorama worthy of Bruegel:

> whence we saw a complete horizon of plain, canals, intersecting
> trees, and houses and steeples thrown here and there, with Gand
> below at our feet. The sea at a distance, bound by the hands of
> man, which pointed 'So far shall ye go and no further.' Bruges

held in the horizon its steeples to our view, and many hamlets raised from out their surrounding wood their single spires to sight.

Throughout the journey, where a French version of a city name exists, Polidori would always adopt it, hence Gand for Ghent, Anvers for Antwerp and even Aix-la-Chapelle for Aachen. This is not only a reflection of his fluency in French but also of a period in history when French rule had just ceased to cover much of Europe.

Making up for the lack of art appreciation in Bruges, Byron and his doctor headed for the Ecole de Dessin, where John complained about the art students blocking his view of Rubens' *St Roch amongst the Sick of Plague*. He admits to being "no connoisseur", although he is happy to venture thoughts on everything from Teniers to van Eyck. With tongue in cheek, he cannot resist an opinion of Netherlandish visual trickery, considering whether "mere deceit is the acme of perfection". He gives us the image of Byron being fooled by a painted board masquerading as a door — so effectively that we see the poet trying to open it. We wonder whether he laughed along or flounced away in a sulk.

Ghent was the birthplace of Charles I of Spain, otherwise known as Charles V, the Holy Roman Emperor who is famously quoted as saying "I speak Spanish to God, Italian to Women, French to Men, and German to my Horse." Whether he actually said these words is open to question, but it does reflect the priorities of the day and his pan-European credentials. Dutch is missing from this list but, to his dying day, he spoke Spanish with a Flemish accent and it was to Ghent he came before retiring in monkish retreat to a monastery in Yuste, Spain in 1556. Polidori uses the phrase, "his last draught of worldly joy" to succinctly capture Charles' trip back to the halcyon days of his youth when the considerable weight of the New World was not on his shoulders. John felt the city was worthy of its illustrious ancestor, crowning his epithets with the conclusion that its streets were the finest he had ever seen.

Contrary to the early nineteenth century, Ghent is now overshadowed by its more compact and prettier neighbour, Bruges. Urban sprawl surrounds the heavy, imposing fortifications and the overhead tram-lines criss-cross in front of the Gothic turrets and gabled houses. Although the city still retains the impression of a rich past and a vibrant present, the twenty-first century tourist's eye is drawn to the more traditional ease of Bruges, set in its museum-like aspic. More authentic in its everyday routine, Ghent has ample time to accommodate the visitor whilst continuing to exist as a working town – a trait it shares with Antwerp.

By now, the local press had got wind of Byron's passage through the Low Countries. John notes in his diary that the Ghent Gazette had written a piece on the poet. Any proto-paparazzi with pad and charcoal would have found it difficult to miss the outsized Napoleonic carriage that had the habit of breaking down. Indeed, Byron and Polidori's grand entrance to Antwerp was marred by a jammed wheel. Gallantly, the doctor rode off in search of assistance. Whilst waiting for repairs to be affected, the group, including servants, descended upon a poor householder where Polidori was, for the first time on this trip, able to use his medical skills on someone else, rather than pandering to the self-absorbed hypochondria of Byron or ministering to his own maladies. He provided some medicine for a fever and pain relief for a toothache. The two daughters of the sickly couple were most grateful but John, rather ungraciously, describes them as "ugly" – adding to his collected commentary on the Flemish face.

Antwerp is on the east bank of the river Scheldt and is the second largest city in modern Belgium. The river-front is guarded by two stone lions that John purposely took a carriage to visit. Beyond the lions, a raised boardwalk contemplates the rather muddy river. As we followed the bank, couples on the benches moved closer in the spirit of intimacy and in search of shelter against the chilling summer wind. The occasional solitary man sat with a beer can and a faraway look, giving the whole area the atmosphere of a seaside resort in the off-season. Things could not have been more different in the centre of the city, where the Grote Markt and Groenplaats form its heart.

The Grote Markt developed in the sixteenth century at the height of Antwerp's power as a trading centre. The characteristic tall merchant houses stand shoulder to shoulder along one side of the square in contrast to the town hall which has a far more Italianate appearance, its ground floor porticoes stretching the length of the building. Byron and Polidori would not have seen the fountain that dominates the square as it was only constructed in the latter half of the nineteenth century. Water splashes down from the heights of the Roman figure, Brabo, who supposedly freed Antwerp from a giant by throwing the colossus' severed hand into the river.

John mentions the architecture but, as was so often the case, he filtered it through the lens of French destruction. The departing Napoleonic troops had left considerable mayhem. In an unnamed chapel of the Cathedral of Our Lady, he gives us a litany of vandalism: defaced roof beams, stolen pictures, column fragments and pilfered marble. It seems the only altar of worth had been saved by a barber who purchased it. Polidori, always alert to the idiosyncratic, was nonplussed to find that Netherlandish barbers represented their establishments with Mambrino's helmet. Perhaps he should not have been that surprised given his previous reference to Charles V.

Ghent, Antwerp and the other cities of the Low Countries had been under Spanish rule and Cervantes' great novel, *Don Quixote*, would have been in wide circulation. In *Quixote*, the eponymous hero mistakes a mere barber's basin for the fictional golden helmet of Moorish king, Mambrino, and embarks on a quest to acquire the basin because he believes it will afford him the magical benefit of invincibility. Ever since, the mythic piece of headwear has been associated with the barbering profession. Antwerp's barbers may have lacked invincibility, but they had enough spare cash to save some of the city's relics from marauding troops.

Not all of the mislaid, broken or stolen religious objects found their way back to the religious institutions they had wandered from. We were walking through Torfbrug, an alleyway behind the commanding Gothic cathedral, when, through a leaded glass window, we spotted the silhouette of a carved Virgin. On closer inspection, other windows were similarly adorned with religious figurines turned inwards. The sacred had met the profane; the establishment in question was a bar. Inside, the ledges and shelves were stocked with robed evangelists, penitent Magdalens, golden virgins and carved crosses. Statues, no longer shadowed by the cloak of their stone niches, looked down on clients swilling the Trappist brews on offer to the patrons. Far from being judgemental, the atmosphere was a human one, life continuing in the age-old tradition of ale, conversation and laughter. Byron would have appreciated the ludicrous juxtaposition of this unique establishment. Polidori, we suspect, would have still been fighting the latent spirit of his Catholic upbringing.

Lured by their own version of the sacrosanct and secular, the pair went in search of the tomb belonging to the painter, Peter Paul Rubens. They found it in the Church of St James, off Lange Nieuwstraat, and his resting place is still as John described it: "It is worthy of him: ornamented by a painting, by himself, of St George, and a statue he brought with him from Rome of the Holy Virgin."

In contrast to these warm feelings for the artist's resting place, Polidori supplied a much chillier comment on a more extensive collection of the painter's works. In John's words, we can hear the echoes of his master's voice and a desire to emulate Byron's antagonistic opinions, rather than being true to the opposing views that he often held on Flemish art. He calls Rubens "a mere dauber in design. There is a *Mary going to Elizabeth*, looking more like a cardinal: indeed, my companion, Lord Byron, took her for one of the red-vested nobles. No divinity about his Christs; putrefaction upon his Gods; exaggerated passion about his men and women".

The painting of the Virgin Mary and her cousin, Elizabeth, forms the left-hand panel of a tryptic called *The Descent from the Cross* and is now located in the cathedral. This early seventeenth-century depiction by Rubens has Mary wearing a bright red tunic and a wide-brimmed black hat, hence the rather juvenile reference to the appearance of a cardinal. Her pregnant figure and fair countenance belie this facile jibe. If we were to be equally facile, we would interpret Elizabeth's quizzical finger pointing to Mary's unborn child as an incredulous gesture that questions the male contribution.

From the cathedral, our duo went to inspect the "Basins" — the dock yards built by Napoleon along the river Scheldt. The Hanseatic trading hall had been commandeered as a weapons' store and all reeked of the recent conflict. Polidori refers to the "Walcheren business" in his diary, a sideways reference to the conflict at the mouth of the Scheldt estuary that saw over 4,000 British soldiers die, not only in battle, but from malaria and typhus. French losses were equally high but did not result from disease.

After lunch on 30 April, Byron's party left the city. Once again, the temperamental carriage broke down and the group had to walk to Malines (Mechelen in Dutch) which considerably lengthened the day. John had enough time to look around and decide that the women had improved. The further away from the coast they travelled, the more Polidori felt the landscape resembled England with its "gentle swells, many pollards and more miserable cottages".

Malines was but a brief interlude *en route* to Brussels where the troublesome transport would receive a much-needed overhaul. John's opinion of the now Belgian capital chimes exactly with ours: "Brussels, the old town, is not so fine as Antwerp, Ghent or Bruges." The small entourage headed for the Hotel d'Angleterre, which used to be in Rue Ducale, a twenty minute stroll from the Grand Place which Polidori calls the Grand Marché, lined with the town hall and the Maison du Roi, the former residence of the country's ruling Spanish monarchs and now the Musée de la Ville. The hotel has morphed into an embassy and bears a small inscription in French which translates as: "In the Spring of 1816, this house sheltered Lord Byron for a few days having left the homeland that disregarded his genius and which he would never see again. Here he composed the stanzas for the third Canto of Childe Harold about the Battle of Waterloo."

Then, as today, Brussels was a beacon of Francophonia amidst a sea of Dutch-speaking Flemish provinces. It was the first time that John's language skills could take full effect, although Byron was proficient enough in French to get by without help. Nevertheless, with an aristocrat's flourish, he very infrequently bothered with trivial arrangements. It was left to John to contact the coach-maker who had been designated to make the necessary repairs.

Having a little more time on his hands than usual, the doctor treated himself to a theatre visit and was shocked by what he saw. The better boxes had already been allotted to season-ticket holders and, on pushing open the door to one that was vacant, he found nothing but filth, rickety chairs and a miniscule chandelier. From this less than salubrious vantage point, he became even more appalled by the entertainments on offer. The production was a farce in more ways than one, and the best of the actresses "spoke French like a base pig". His attention was only held by the many English ladies he had discovered, whom he considered "the only good-looking women in Brussels".

At this point, it is worth quoting Polidori at length as he vents his spleen on the inhabitants of the city:

> It is not for a foreigner to call a thing absurd because it does not tally well with ideas, or the ladies' costume, except the black mantle, should be put down as such by me. The men are also short and bad-looking, either consummate impudence or complete insignificance – no individuality. The indelicacy of these Belgians is gross; all kind of disgusting books publicly sold, and exposed to the eyes of all young damsels – beastliness publically exhibited on the public monuments – fountains with men vomiting with effort a stream of water – and still worse.

This outpouring of scathing criticism does not put John in the best of lights and represents one of the least appealing aspects of his character. Not having been born into the aristocracy and, essentially, a foreigner in his own land, he had taken this opportunity to elevate his own sense of self-worth by denigrating those around him whose standards he considered less commendable than his own. The words "complete insignificance" are telling, as this is precisely the feeling he would have in the orbit of Byron and Shelley during the summer to come in Switzerland.

Putting aside Polidori's prejudices, there is an undeniable corporality to the city's statuary. We are all aware of Hiëronymus Duquesnoy the Elder's *Manneken Pis*, the naked little boy who is doomed to piss for posterity into the fountain below, but perhaps the most curious monument of all commemorates the vomit of Russian Tsar, Peter the Great. John did mention spewing statues, but he was too early to have witnessed the commemoration of such royal outpourings.

In the Parc de Bruxelles, there are two pits on either side of the central path, which were left to their natural formation when the rest of the park was landscaped in the English fashion. Despite the salubrious residences surrounding the greenery, this area has something of a reputation for late-night revelry and other urban mischief, including prostitution. It seems that, back in 1717, Peter the Great had been wandering these environs in the mid-afternoon, suffering the effects of the night before.

His guide witnessed the Russian empty the contents of his stomach into a nearby fountain and the anecdote passed down the ages until a certain Prince Demidoff donated a statue of the Tsar in 1856. This would be largely unremarkable if it were not for the fact he included an inscription in Latin: INSIDENS MARCINI FONTIS AQUAM ILLUS NOBILTAVIT LIBATO VINO, which loosely translated means 'He sat on the rim of this fountain and graced its waters with the wine of his libations'. After wandering around the plinth several times and checking our location, we could find no hint of the regurgitated Latin. A passerby, obviously used to puzzled visitors, told us that the basin harbouring the inscription had long since been removed by certain denizens of the area.

Had the statue existed in 1816, it might have been visible from the windows of Byron's room in the neighbouring d'Angleterre, as the Rue Ducale borders the park. The poet was finding Brussels a tiresome interruption in his journey as the transport issues multiplied. The Belgian coachmaker who had, in fact, made the original carriage for Napoleon, was now criticizing the London workmanship which had led to the locking front wheels. Byron dashed off a missive to Hobhouse, asking his friend to abuse said craftsman "like a pickpocket". This is rich, indeed, as Byron had not paid a penny for the considerable expense of creating such a white elephant. It was John's task to sort out an alternative *calèche* but, lacking business acumen, Polidori found himself overpaying; however, at least they were able to take an excursion to Waterloo.

The name still resonates through the centuries as the defining battle of the Napoleonic era. Given its historical importance, we had imagined that it would have escaped the ravages of modern development. This is partly true, but a motorway has sliced through the field and cars hurtle past the commemorative Butte de Lion every minute of every day. The Butte is a conical earthen mound topped with a cast-iron lion, marking the point at which Wellington's Dutch general, the Prince of Orange, was injured. It provides a panoramic view of the battlefield that was not available to Byron and Polidori, who visited ten years before its construction and less than a year after the battle had finished.

The Duke of Wellington's troops, consisting of soldiers from the Low Countries, Germany and Britain, eventually overcame Bonaparte's army when the remaining units at La Belle Alliance were routed and forced to withdraw. Napoleon even left jewels and a carriage behind in his rush to escape. The artefacts from the battle are now safely housed in the Musée Wellington in the hamlet of Waterloo and at Napoleon's Last Headquarters, the farmhouse of Le Caillou, also a museum. Both have their rather macabre exhibits – the former is home to Lord Uxbridge's artificial leg which replaced the one severed by a cannon on the battlefield, whilst the latter contains a death mask of the Emperor.

Polidori's description of their visit is extensive and with events having been so recent, the ghosts of slain soldiers are almost visible. Battle artefacts were then in the hands of locals keen to sell ghoulish souvenirs to anyone visiting the site. On first arriving, the pair were inundated by ragamuffins trying to flog anything from regimental books to uniform buttons. It was also not uncommon for visitors to discover human remains – a disembodied hand in the woods or a booted foot hidden in the grass. The whole process of protecting the battlefield was undertaken in an effort to keep at bay the roving gangs of looters. Educated men, like Byron, were more than happy to take away blood-stained letters and clothing perforated with the implements of death.

Initially, the poet seemed subdued, whether out of reverence or temper, it would be impossible to say. He was no admirer of Wellington or his reactionary politics and had even lost a cousin, Frederick Howard, in the battle. Despite having previously quarrelled with Howard, he requested a guide to show him the place where his relative had fallen. Polidori respectfully followed in Byron's wake recording the sombre details. At Hougoumont, the farm shelled heavily by the French, John puts himself in the position of the attacking Napoleonic troops:

"Indeed, the gallantry, the resolution and courage, which the French displayed in attacking this place, guarded from the heights by our cannon, and by our soldiers through the loop-holes, would alone ennoble the cause in which they fought." The only part of the farm to survive was the chapel, where "the fire consumed the toes of a crucifix". The doctor and the poet left their names in remembrance.

La Belle Alliance, the scene of the beginning of the end, is where Wellington met the Prussian commander, Gebhard Leberecht von Blücher, Prince of Wahlstatt. Polidori informs us that the *alliance* in question was a matrimonial one and that the name was a pure coincidence. Unable to resist the lure of the physicality of war any longer, the pair purchased "helms, cuirasses, swords, etc., of an officer and soldier of cuirasses, besides eagles, cockades, etc.".

As dusk fell, it only remained for a final Byronic flourish which is the one image of Waterloo many associate with the man who penned "And Harold stands upon this place of skulls, / The grave of France, the deadly Waterloo!". Without fanfare, Byron jumped on his steed and galloped at full tilt across the battlefield singing Turkish war songs at the top of his voice. Polidori cantered hard behind in silence but bursting with the romanticism of the occasion.

Aside from the assorted weaponry, Byron also purchased a blood-spattered pocketbook belonging to a French infantryman. The sad little *memento mori* had the details of its former owner, a certain Louis Marie Joseph Mounsigny from Dondouville. These details personalize the enormity and anonymity of death on a large scale – the fallen had names, families and possessions. The chilling thought of owning something covered with the blood that seeped from the veins of this dying man is little diminished by the centuries.

John was wrenched back to the reality of his existence when he was given the job of bundling up the souvenirs for shipment back to the poet's publisher, John Murray, and entrusting Murray to pay any customs duty due. A further dose of mundanity arrived with the realization that the new *calèche* was not as roadworthy as it had seemed. John implies that the coach was "jogged", that is to say 'unsteady' and tried to return it to the owner who wanted to keep a substantial proportion of the deposit. To the rescue came Pryse Lockhart Gordon, a family friend of Byron's and a writer who would go on to author *A Companion to Italy*. Currently residing in Brussels, he offered to take the carriage off their hands.

Polidori may have thought that Gordon had taken to him, presented as he was with a copy of the works of Giovanni Battista Casti, although clearly the draw was Lord Byron – as we can see when Gordon called to ask the pair to take coffee with him: "We went, and were graciously received; Lord B as himself, I as a tassel to the purse of merit." This statement carries the weight of authenticity and a recognition of their true relationship. This was a position he was not prepared to admit to his sister, Frances, in a letter he sent from Brussels dated 2 May.

> I am very pleased with Lord Byron. I am with him on the footing of an equal, everything alike; at present here we have a suite of rooms between us. I have my sitting-room at one end, he at the other. He has not shown any passion; though we have had nothing but a series of mishaps that have put me out of temper though they have not ruffled his. The carriage, the new carriage, has had three stoppages. We are at present at Brussels merely to have the carriage-part well looked at and repaired.

He signs off the letter with an enquiry about "Papa, Mamma, Meggy (have you heard from her?), Charlotte, Bob, Henry, Eliza and Mr Deagostini". Therein lays the deceit of the above paragraph as he knew all would be reported to his disapproving father.

The trouble with the carriage rumbled on and Byron's dispute over money made the papers, specifically the *Courier*, which reported the untrustworthiness of the poet. Before leaving the city and, we suspect, to avoid attention, the party took an excursion to Chateau du Lac, otherwise known as Laeken, where Napoleon had been an occupant. The Castle is now the official residence of the King of Belgium. As they returned, the weather set in and rain pummelled the badly paved tracks. The gods were whispering their ill-omens.

In his more lucid moments, our doctor knew his status, but his youth, pride and eagerness would often blind him to the truth. He found the lie more comforting than the reality. Had he known that Byron found little interest in his rambling discourses on lotions, potions and poisons, he would have been dismayed. For now, ignorance was bliss and permitted the journey to continue in a more or less harmonious manner.

Byron and his entourage left Brussels on 6 May and headed for Liège via St Trond (Sint Truiden). As they passed into Wallonia, the French-speaking area, there was a noticeable decline in the standards of the rural dwellings ("dung hills at their doors, and ditches with black fetid water before their first step"). Wallonia was only just beginning to capitalize on its coal and iron deposits which gave it a period of unprecedented growth later in the nineteenth century, followed by the kind of decline experienced by similar areas in the north of England.

By now, the aristocrat had seen enough of the Low Countries and was in a hurry to reach the Rhine and turn towards the south. The landscape is more varied in this part of Belgium with the appearance of hills and valleys that are easily negotiated in modern transport but which left Polidori feeling nauseous as the coach rocked on its new springs. To further dampen the mood, every stopping point saw a plague of urchins begging for alms. Byron felt the need to pause and recover before heading into Germany; the doctor, increasingly irritated by the pace, was all for pushing on whilst the wheels of the carriage were still in working order.

CHAPTER THREE

The Rhine
Seduced by Loreley

The Belgian town of Battice would prove a turning point in Polidori and Byron's journey. The clouds were beginning to gather, the changeable weather a reflection of a darkening turn in their incipient relationship. As rain fell into the roadside ponds, only to be obliterated by sporadic sunshine, Polidori persuaded Byron, after some heated debate, to head for Aix-la-Chapelle – now more commonly known as Aachen. Rather than spending some time recuperating in Battice, the pair headed for the city newly acquired by the Prussians. The carriage-ride was their worst yet, "jolting, rolling, knocking" them into a foul temper.

Although Polidori clearly had little notion of the pitted pathway that would lie before them, he shouldered the blame as Byron openly accused him of giving bad advice. These were also tumultuous times for the city of Aachen, as it had ceased to be a free imperial city of the Holy Roman Empire in 1794. It was to pass to the French, only to be ceded to the Prussians less than a year before the arrival of our two travellers. Fortunately, for the sake of harmony, they decided to leave each other to their own devices and explore the city independently.

John stoutly refers to the settlement as "Aix-la-Chapelle" and continued to use his fluent French, not infrequently being mistaken for a Frenchman. He was not always understood, however, and had to resort to his self-confessed "broken German". It is in such a manner that he asked for directions to the mineral baths and was led by a young lad to an establishment that John found lacking in hygiene. Paterson's 1886 *Guide to the Rhine* remarks that the water "contains a larger proportion of sulphur than any other spring in Europe. It is also

Drachenfels near Königswinter, Ricco Stange, Pixabay

Castle Frankenstein, Burg Frankenstein, Lapping, PIxabay

The Rhine at
Bingen, A. Edwards

The tomb of General
Lahmberg, Mainz
Cathedral, S.
Edwards

strongly impregnated with sulphuretted hydrogen gas, which gives it a strong taste and odour".

This description chimes, almost identically, with Polidori's who assures us that the actual sulphur beds were only shown to aristocrats and monarchs, sarcastically writing that "a kingdom is good for something". No doubt, in the eighty years between John's visit and the publishing of Paterson's guidebook, the Kaiserbad had been somewhat smartened up. Those taking the waters to find a cure in the latter half of the nineteenth century were chiefly seeking to alleviate the socially acceptable pain of rheumatism. Earlier visitors would have been desperate to calm the symptoms of syphilis. One can only imagine the stew created by large quantities of syphilitic bathers.

Aachen takes its very name from the Old Germanic *ahha* referring to 'water' or a 'stream'. It is no surprise that bathing has a long history in the city and even in the unwashed Middle-Ages Aachen was unusual in continuing the tradition thanks to Charlemagne, the famed King of the Franks and first Holy Roman Emperor. He spent much of the last twenty years of his life, from 792, wintering in the town, occasionally swimming in its hot springs. It was only in the Renaissance when the healing properties of thermal waters sparked renewed interest that the springs further developed. The wonderfully named Franciscus Fabricius Ruremundanus was Aachen's promoter-in-chief.

Bathing culture was at its height in the eighteenth and nineteenth centuries and a proto-tourist industry developed alongside it, with evenings full of galas, balls, theatre and other amusements. Under the category of other amusements was the city's surprising reputation as one of the foremost capitals for those in search of the pleasures of the flesh. Prostitution was rife from the middle of the seventeenth century and continued in the same vein until well after Polidori's visit. Visitors who dabbled with *les dames publiques* often found themselves returning to ease their syphilis.

John provides us with an interesting insight into the area's attitude to the recently departed French and its more risqué reputation on leaving Aachen for Jülich. He admitted to being swayed by an attractive local woman's opinion: "on my asking her whether the *dames n'aimaient pas beaucoup les Français*, answered, '*Oui, les dames publiques.*'" No doubt the French soldiers were regular visitors.

The modern-day guest needs little in the way of direction to the waters, apart from a sense of smell. A tourist walking down Hartmannstrasse from the cathedral in Münsterplatz will be drawn by the increasingly pungent odour of sulphur from the Elisenbrunnen, a fountain and white porticoed hall that provides access to the thermal springs. Constructed a mere 11 years after Polidori and Byron strode the same streets, the Elisenbrunnen bears witness to centuries of illustrious visitors via the plaques on its walls; names include Händel and Casanova.

Inevitably, Polidori's attention was also drawn by the Aachener Dom, the cathedral constructed on the order of Charlemagne in 796. In terms of art, we have already become accustomed to John's more sure-footed opinions as opposed to Byron's high-minded flippancy. However, on this occasion, the doctor failed to grasp the importance of the oldest cathedral in northern Europe and its Byzantine influence, a later, albeit less ornate, mirror of the Basilica of San Vitale in Ravenna. Polidori dismisses the building and its worshippers with this off-hand remark: "full of people, lower ranks, hearing mass. Miserable painting, architecture, etc."

It is difficult to believe that John, the Catholic-educated student of many disciplines, was blind to the dramatic effect of the octagon at the heart of the structure. Two storeys of piers support an octagonal layer with a window in each side, crowned by the magnificent gold cupola. The whole effect is punctuated by the Barbarossa chandelier, commissioned by yet another famous Holy Roman Emperor, Frederick I, who was elected to his seat in 1152. The impressive copper wheel-shaped chandelier incorporates 48 candles which are still lit when the occasion demands.

It is true that much of the cathedral has been altered over the years with additions to the outer decoration and the fading of the crushed red-brick plaster. The inside of the cupola was even stuccoed during the Baroque period and not reproduced in its current splendour until the nineteenth century, for which we can give Polidori the benefit of the doubt.

John's diary details his exit from Aachen through "a fine country, with no hedges but fine woods in the distance", but he becomes somewhat confused in his chronology and makes a further reference to Battice, which he and Byron had argued over before entering the German-speaking lands. If the timeline is a little disordered, the point he makes is startlingly clear, even to the modern reader. As he passed from the Netherlandish regions into Prussia, he had this to say: "It causes a strange sensation to an Englishman to pass into one state from another without crossing any visible line."

Like so many used to criss-crossing borders in Europe with ease, we made the same journey from Belgium to Germany noticing little change except subtle alterations in landscape and, when buildings appeared, a characteristic refocusing of architecture, as well as the obvious language differences on the road signs. Such a soft blending of countries has created a mindset that some in Britain still find hard to understand when the English Channel yawns between the Kent coast and the continent.

Polidori and Byron's arrival at their next destination of note, Cologne, has a surprising abruptness. The pair spent time lamenting their inability to see the city and the spires of its cathedral, supposedly visible from some distance, only to find themselves "suddenly under its battlements and towers". The same could not be said of John Cam Hobhouse, Byron's closest friend, who undertook a very similar journey with Scrope Davies, later in the same year, with the aim of meeting up with the poet at his rented summer residence of Villa Diodati on the shores of Lake Geneva. Hobhouse was aware of the cathedral long before he entered the city, spotting its distinctive outline as his carriage "jog trotted" through the corn fields on the banks of the Rhine.

Although the cathedral's spires still dominate the skyline, their full extension is a nineteenth-century addition; the angle of approach to the city determines the moment at which they become visible, even more so in the twenty-first century as the multi-storeyed edifices of modern Cologne compete with its medieval masterpiece. Johann Wolfgang von Goethe, a contemporary and admirer of Byron, likened the German Gothic cathedral to "a sublimely towering wide-spreading tree of God" of which Cologne is perhaps the best example, being, at one time, the tallest structure in the world.

The art historian, Andrew Graham-Dixon, has described Cologne cathedral as encapsulating the schizophrenic nature of German art, veering from the refined and delicate to the mysterious and Gothic. Like Graham-Dixon, we also discovered the wooden choirstalls with the carved grotesques seemingly peering from the forest floor of a dark Germanic wood. Roman authors, notably Tacitus, were some of the first to mention the influence of the mysterious forest and its shadowy portents on the German soul. The architecture of St Peter's in Cologne is not so very far removed from the hill of Drachenfels and Burg Frankenstein which Polidori and Byron will shortly pass and the Shelleys had previously seen in 1814.

The cathedral, bordering the Domplatte and, more prosaically, the Hauptbahnhof (central station) stretches steeply skywards, its darkened façade not a reflection of its Gothic origins but the consequence of centuries of pollution. The colour, however, adds to its brooding quality and massive presence. Inside, it was not the wooden carving but the glories of the stained glass that drew Polidori's attention: "The effect of its being very high and variegated in the choir is beautiful."

Much of the stained glass that we see today is not that which so awed Polidori owing to its destruction during the Second World War; although, there is an echo of this in John's words as he highlights the devastation wrought by Napoleonic troops: "the roof of the nave obliged to be restored with plain board – a staring monument over Gallic ruin". Let us not forget that the only reason Byron chose a route down the Rhine was to avoid the messy aftermath of Napoleonic rule in France, with its restored retrograde regime.

Reunited in their sightseeing endeavours, the poet and doctor proceeded to the Shrine of the Three Kings – a large golden reliquary situated behind the high altar and said to contain the bones of the Three Wise Men. Polidori assures us of its monetary value rather than its spiritual worth. The boy, who, when at Ampleforth College in Yorkshire, once expressed the vague aim of becoming a priest, was now clearly rooted in secular values. The world-weary influence of Byron, although he never professed the atheism of Shelley, was bound to influence the impressionable young physician.

As the party moved away from the treasury, Polidori tripped on a step and his subsequent fall broke a glass. Fortunately, it was not a priceless item and he eventually persuaded the church authorities to take three francs in payment. This incident is but the first in what would prove to be a litany of physical mishaps. Despite his boyish glamour and dandified appearance, Polidori had a nervous excitability that led to the kind of clumsiness that would see him sprain an ankle during the fateful days of story-telling over the Genevan summer.

On the appropriately named Ursulaplatz, beyond the station, is the Church of St Ursula, a Romanesque structure with a seventeenth-century baroque interior. As a plaque on the wall testifies, the structure would have been in a parlous state at the time of John's visit; only subsequent renovation has given it the neat, sandy coloured brickwork and fresh appearance that it now possesses. The wall of the southern aisle is adorned with representations of ten of the apostles dating back to 1224, some of the earliest examples from the so-called German School.

The sides of the church are also lined with heavy-lidded sarcophagi lending the atmosphere a sombre note, even without the prior knowledge that a golden chamber will shortly add to the aura of death. A wall confronts the visitor which, on first sight, resembles a collage of wheat woven into an inscripted design; peer closer and the enormity of its actual composition becomes clear. The vision of wheat crystallizes into a façade of bones – femurs, scapulae, clavicles, ribs and vertebrae – the skulls being reserved for special attention in lantern-like ossuaries. We can read in Polidori's breathless account the impact of this macabre art:

> Went to see St Ursula's Church, where we were shown virgins'
> skulls of ninety years old, male and female, all jumbled into a
> mass of 11,000 virgins' bones arranged all in order – some gilt,
> etc. A whole room bedecked with them. All around, indeed,
> whatever we saw were relics, skulls; some in the head of silver-
> faced busts, some arranged in little cells with velvet cases,
> wherein was worked the name of each.

John, in a Byronesque touch, asked to remove a small piece from the mass of decayed humanity, only to be referred to a Latin interdiction which he nonchalantly tells us he did not bother to read. The deep impression of such a sight may well have rested in his subconscious only to re-emerge in his first attempt at writing a ghost story at the Villa Diodati. Mary Shelley recalled that Polidori's initial draft had the theme of a skull-headed lady who was punished for looking through a keyhole, although the veracity of this has been disputed, especially given Polidori was writing *Ernestus Berchtold* at the time.

In fact, John's enthusiasm had slightly misinterpreted the legend of St Ursula. The majority of the relics were found in the ground on which the current church stands; supposedly, they represent St Ursula and her coterie of virgins. In Britain, in the fifth century, a pre-Christian king Vionutus and his wife were childless and were prompted to convert to Christianity with the promise of offspring. The subsequent daughter, Ursula, refused all suitors until similar divine intervention suggested she marry Conan of Cologne in order to convert his populace.

She left for the city accompanied by the famous 11,000 virgins by way of a detour to Rome as a pilgrimage. Before the marriage could take place, Cologne was swamped by an army of invading Huns and the many virgins would have been easy prey for the licentious troops if they had not stoutly refused to co-operate. As a consequence, they were all massacred and buried where they fell. Documents from the seventh and eighth centuries indicate that the bones began to emerge and be venerated as saintly objects; especially the body of St Ursula said to have been uncovered by St Cunibert. Perhaps the significantly overestimated number of 11,000 is due to the fact that one of the virgins bore the name *Undecimmillia*, meaning 11,000. However, scientists have identified over 3,000 individual skulls of young women that show a violent death, not all of which are in the golden chamber.

Polidori's taste for art, inspired by the work he had already encountered, was shortly to be widened further after leaving the Gothic atmosphere of the churches behind. Independently of Byron, he sent a letter of introduction to a certain Franz Ferdinand Wallraf, the owner of the city's most significant private collection of paintings. Our doctor even notes that the elderly gentleman intended to leave his collection to Cologne upon his death, which indeed he did in 1824. John is frustratingly scant in his references to the paintings, name dropping Poussin, Claude Lorrain, Tintoretto and Rembrandt, among others. The museum has moved site to Obenmarspforten and expanded, with many acquisitions made or donations received since the death of the venerable Wallraf, including some of the names mentioned.

Certainly, Polidori would have seen the *Martyrdom of St Ursula at Cologne*, with the story already familiar to him from the church. Painted by the anonymous Master of the Little Passion in around 1400, it formed part of Wallraf's personal collection and depicts the medieval walled city, complete with religious institutions and fortifications. In the foreground, boats approach from the river with Ursula and some of her virgins aboard, whilst others are being cruelly attacked on the periphery.

John was also impressed by a Terniers, namely a David Teniers the Younger which typically details a Flemish street scene of chatting peasants and a thatched cottage. Delighted as Wallraf was to show off his pictures, his main topic of conversation seems to have been the loss of much artwork in the recent French attacks. To illustrate his point, he took a torn leaf from a church missal and brandished it in front of Polidori saying how many had gone missing from places of worship. The hidden agenda in conversing with his new Anglo-Italian acquaintance was to make use of his contacts in London to track down a copy of Caxton's printing.

If it proved difficult to place ourselves before the exact pictures gazed upon by the elderly collector and his enthusiastic young visitor, it was even more problematic to locate the Hotel de Prague where Byron and his entourage stayed when they found other inns at full capacity. Typically, Polidori gives the name in French, but the building was more commonly known as the Pragerhof. An old print by Samuel Prout shows it as an ornate building with a conical window structure topped by a tiled roof extending to a point. The neighbouring archway is backed by a hexagonal tower that pierces the skyline. The Pragerhof was in the Neumarkt and the feature that gives away its location is the still-remaining tower that looms over the archless street corner of Richmodstrasse. The tower displays a plaque claiming its historical significance as the birthplace of composer Max Bruch.

Before checking out of the hotel, the doctor went in search of books which were almost never of a medical nature but rather works to feed his literary ambitions. He mentions a Miss Helmhoft in his diary with no further context given except the fact that she was a lover of German poetry and happy to read some verses to an uncomprehending Polidori, whose polite laughter at her gestures was mistaken for an appreciation of the poet's wit.

John's farewell to Cologne sees him at last mention the Rhine, a river that will accompany him and Byron all the way to Switzerland and provide his illustrious employer with what the Irish poet, Thomas Moore, would call "a line of road which he had strewed over with all the riches of poesy". Before Byron left England, Moore had almost resorted to fisticuffs with the aristocrat over a slur he had made regarding an empty pistol and a duel that Moore had intended to fight in an attempt to defend his poetic condemnation of the United States.

Moore subsequently met Byron in Geneva and the pair settled their differences to such a degree that they became firm friends. The Irishman received Byron's memoirs in Venice, only to be one of the infamous gathering who burnt them in order to supposedly preserve what was left of the poet's reputation after he had died. Moore did, however, produce a *Life of Lord Byron*, interspersed with his letters and journals from which the above quote has been taken.

For someone who could so readily turn a scene before him into "poesy", the Rhine valley was indeed fertile ground. Not for nothing did Samuel Taylor Coleridge describe Byron as a "Picturesque Tourist" who "must be troubled with a mental Strangury, if he could not lift up his leg six times at six different Corners, and each time piss a Canto". Polidori refers to the most famous example of the verses composed by Byron at this time in his 13 May diary entry, lines which would become 'The Castle Crag of Drachenfels' in the third canto of *Childe Harold*.

The pair approached the castle after a fleeting stop in Bonn. The landscape starts to offer the romantic hues captured by writers upon the sight of the Siebengebirge or Seven Mountains, the most storied of which is the eponymous Drachenfels. Today, the castle ruins and late nineteenth-century addition are easily accessible via a rack and pinion railway that takes visitors to the summit from the neighbouring town of Königswinter, the birthplace of the poet Wolfgang Müller in the very year of 1816. He invoked his beloved local landscape in the poem 'Mein Herz ist am Rhein' ('My heart is by the Rhine') published in the 1870s anthology, *Dichtungen eines rheinischen Poeten* (*Poesies of a Rhine poet*). Müller's work is imbued with the beauty and legends of the river, with Drachenfels not lacking in either.

The Dragon Mountain, as it is most appropriately translated in English, has a cavern where its fire-breathing inhabitant was supposed to dwell. The legend is recounted in the *Lay of the Nibelungs* and features no less a hero than Siegfried, sent to burn charcoal on the mountain:

> When he upon the mountain erstwhile the dragon slew, in the brute's blood he bathed him, the goodly warrior and since that day, in battle, no steel can cut him more. Yet, no less am I anxious when he in fight doth stand and javelins fly around him from many a hero's hand, lest by mischance I lose him, and mourn my husband dear. Alas, what sorrow have I for Siegfried's sake to bear!

The young warrior neglected to cover with the dragon's blood one small spot on his body, through which he would sadly receive the wound that killed him. There is also a more religious version of the dragon-slaying story that involves the appeasement of the creature through the sacrifice of a Christian maiden, later to become St Margaret. As the dragon awoke from a night's slumber, he spied Margaret strapped to a tree trunk at the entrance to his cave. She held her cross before him causing the monster to yell to the heavens and fall over the cliff only to be impaled on the rocks below.

Adding to the drama is the ruin itself. Originally instituted by Archbishop Frederick I of Cologne in 1111, the structure was intended as a stronghold against Henry V and the robber barons of the vicinity. To avoid conflict, the castle was eventually handed to the Counts of

Drachenfels who gained their wealth by using the mountain to quarry stone for the cathedral of Cologne. The parlous state of the structure which lends it such a brooding air is chiefly due to incursions by the Swedes during the Thirty Years' War.

The view from the summit sweeps down to the Rhine as it flows towards the steeper gorges of myth beyond Koblenz. Polidori, in beholding the views on offer, was awed by the scenery: "We had the river on one side when rose hills (not mountains) cultivated halfway for vines – and the rest, nuts, shrubs, oak, etc. Towers on pinnacles, in ruin; villages (with each its spire) built of mud." It would be true to say that at this juncture, even allowing for the disagreement over road conditions, Polidori was also still in awe of Lord Byron as a poet and person, an opinion no doubt enhanced by this stanza:

> The castled crag of Drachenfels
> Frowns o'er the wide and winding Rhine,
> Whose breast of waters broadly swells
> Between the banks which bear the vine;
> And hills all rich with blossom'd trees,
> And fields which promise corn and wine.
> And scattered cities crowning these,
> Whose far white walls along them shine,
> Have strew'd a scene which I should see
> With double joy wert thou with me.

The "thou" refers to Byron's half-sister, Augusta Leigh. John knew these lines were written for her as he notes "LB wrote to Mrs Leigh some days ago: written May 11 on Rhine-banks". Less clear, however, is the extent to which the doctor knew of the nature of the relationship between the poet and Augusta. Perhaps his youthful enthusiasm and keenness to accompany Byron had made him deaf to the rumours flying around Regency London, although it is hard to believe that they failed to make any impact. As we know, everything from sodomy, hypochondria, cruelty and crucially, incest, were hurled in Byron's direction. Most modern-day biographers acknowledge there is a good deal of truth to the fact that Byron's relationship with his sister went further than a simple meeting of minds.

In 1911, when Polidori's diary was first published posthumously by his nephew, William Michael Rossetti, the self-same Rossetti added footnotes of his own to further explain people, places and certain ambiguities. In one such, he mentions a Mrs Trevanion supposedly belonging to the same Trevanions who featured in the life of Medora Leigh, Augusta's daughter "ostensibly of her husband, but who is now said to have been in fact the daughter of Byron himself". Byron's estranged wife was convinced enough of his paternity to tell her own daughter with the poet, Ada Lovelace, that Medora was her half-sister.

Returning to Polidori's diary and picking up the journey forced by the scandal of these events, we continue along the Rhine to Andernach, occasionally spelt with a terminal 't' on road signs. Our own entrance to the town was punctuated by the "massy towers" that attracted John. These medieval fortifications remain largely intact, incorporating the Stadtmauer (protective wall), two gates, Round Tower and the archiepiscopal castle ruins built by the Electorate of Cologne under the Holy Roman Empire.

Parking requirements directed us to an underground car park in the centre of town. The exit stairs that bring you to the surface had the effect of hurling us into the environs of a twenty-first century shopping mall, hitherto hidden by the medieval approach, giving the surreal impression that we had reappeared in a different town. Happily, the mall emptied us into Hochstrasse, a street that our two nineteenth-century travellers would have recognized with its gable-ended houses and facades bowing under the weight of history. One yellow frontage leans backwards, squeezed by the sagging bones of its elderly orange and red neighbours.

Honoré de Balzac set a short story in Andernach called *L'Auberge rouge* (The Red Inn). In an echo of events at Villa Diodati, Fanny, a banker's daughter asks a dinner guest, Hermann, a German businessman, to tell all assembled a terrifying story. The ensuing tale revolves around two French medical students who stay at the Red Inn of the title. The Andernacher inn-keeper offers the pair his own room which they subsequently agree to share with a German latecomer who carries much wealth. In the night, one of the Frenchmen, Prosper, is tempted to kill the German for his money, only to refrain at the last minute. To his horror, he awakes in the morning to find the wealthy merchant decapitated and his friend missing. He is arrested and imprisoned. It is in prison that Hermann, captured by Napoleonic troops, meets the fateful Prosper and hears his story, before the Frenchman is executed. In a complicated twist, another guest at the original dinner party has fallen in love with the daughter of a rich contractor, also present, who may or may not have been Prosper's missing friend and the perpetrator of the above crime.

Andernach's other literary connection is surprisingly with an American beat poet, one Heinrich Karl Bukowski (commonly known as Charles), who was the son of a German-American father stationed in the town and a local girl with whom he had an affair and subsequently married. Bukowski was born in a house on Atkienstrasse in 1920, moving to the United States three years later as his father found he was unable to make a living. An upbringing in a German-speaking household left Bukowski with a pronounced accent as a child for which he was bullied adding to the physical abuse he also suffered from his father.

The Napoleonic connection featured in Balzac's story is also mentioned by Polidori who pithily remarks that "B's name is everywhere. Who did this? NB. – Who that? – He". The B, of course, is Bonaparte and John is alluding to Napoleon's famous self-aggrandizement. Both Polidori and especially, Byron, had a far from simple relationship with the events of the French Revolution and its aftermath. Given the destruction they had both already seen – the damage to Cologne Cathedral, the battlefield of Waterloo – they were far from ardent enemies of the French.

Byron, being firmly against any form of oppression, was initially in favour of the French Revolution. He was given the epithet "the arch-apostle of revolt" by Albert Hancock in his book *The French Revolution and the English Poets*. However, Byron, in contrast to Shelley, never supported his opinions with serious ideology, resorting to the cynical detestation of all governments that wielded tyrannical power. Recalling Polidori's visit to Waterloo and the Chateau du Lac with his employer, it is interesting to note that they were impressed with the Emperor's castle and John was keen to sit down in two chairs that

Napoleon would have used. The imperial eagles still decorated the furniture and he remarks in his diary that a servant present "seemed a little astonished at our bowing before them".

Mirroring the travels of French Revolutionary troops, the pair moved on to Koblenz, specifically following the path trodden by François Séverin Marceau-Desgraviers, the French General who is buried on the edge of the Volkspark. John placed the tomb a mile from the settlement but it is now firmly within the boundaries of urban Koblenz and shows the degree to which the city has expanded in the last 200 years. According to the doctor, it was a trifle dark, which it is, a pyramid-shaped obelisk in black stone with a mournful lion at its centre.

Once again, Byron could not resist the lure of the romantic figure, fighting for the rights of the common people, as witnessed by more stanzas in Childe Harold:

> By Coblentz, on a rise of gentle ground,
> There is a small and simple pyramid,
> Crowning the summit of the verdant mound;
> Beneath its base are heroes' ashes hid,
> Our enemy's – but let not that forbid
> Honour to Marceau! o'er whose early tomb
> Tears, big tears, gush'd from the rough soldier's lid,
> Lamenting and yet envying such a doom,
> Falling for France, whose rights he battled to resume.

The Byron entourage ate in the Trois Suisses, an inn that had witnessed, according to Polidori, a cannon ball puncturing its walls whilst Marceau was inside. An 1880 print depicts the hotel as a Rhine-side establishment, a splendid four-storeyed building quietly dominating its quayside neighbours as it regards the "flying bridge" of Polidori's description, seemingly supported by nothing more than its tetherings at either side of the bank. From the balconies of the hotel's upper tier, the fortunate guests would have been afforded John's "fine view" of the Ehrenbreitstein fortress sitting high on a hilltop across the river.

Constructed by Ehrenbert in around 1000, the stronghold was reinforced in the sixteenth century in an attempt to make it impregnable to the cannon. As we can see from our doctor's diary, the fortification was not altogether successful, despite repelling the French on three occasions. The views, however, had a greater impact on his writing:

> Went to Ehrenbreitstein. Everything broken by gunpowder; immense masses of solid stone and mortar thrown fifty yards from their original situation; ruined walls, gateways, and halls – nothing perfect. Splendid views thence – Coblentz, Rhine, Moselle with its bridge, mountains, cultivation, vines, wilderness, everything below my feet.

It was the 1794 attack by French troops that must have prompted the removal of the Holy Tunic, a relic guarded by the Trier See that is purported to have been a robe worn by Jesus before his crucifixion. During our visitors' sojourn in the area, the Prussians were just beginning to reinforce Ehrenbreitstein, turning it into the fortress we know today. It survived both World Wars intact, and still commands beautiful views over the Rhine, eulogized by Herman Melville in his Gothic-inspired novel of family tension, *Pierre*: "As the vine flourishes, and the grape empurples close up to the very walls and muzzles of cannoned Ehrenbreitstein; so do the sweetest joys of life grow in the very jaws of its perils."

The scholar, Merton M. Sealts, produced a 1988 volume, *Melville's Reading*, which focussed on the texts that influenced the writer of *Moby Dick*. We should not be surprised that among the works we find the poetry of Lord Byron and Sealts goes as far as to suggest that Byron provided the model for his character Pierre, specifically in the first three chapters of the book. The plot contains a long-lost half-sister, fears of incest, inheritance, a ménage-a-trois and tragedy. It does sound remarkably similar to Byron's escape to exile and events that unfolded later in the summer.

Melville uses the delicious adjective "empurples" to describe the ripening of the grapes, although this is the home of Riesling, a white grape variety originating in an area that now has UNESCO World Heritage status. Polidori made the sweeping statement on 11 May that at "Andernach the Rhine loses much"; he was soon to realize, in fact, that the flattening of land prior to the town was but a precursor to the spectacular gorges, laced with vines, that exemplify the river from Koblenz to Bingen, and he found the "scenery sublime".

It is at this point that a celebrated incident may or may not have taken place. John, for the first time, went out on the river in a boat, resembling an "Otaheitan" canoe, which was rowed by an unnamed oarsman. The only source for our possibly apocryphal story is Thomas Moore, although Moore swears that Byron used to recount the tale himself. Milord was evidently on board the same canoe and was asked by Polidori, "'What is there you can do that I cannot?'" It seems Bryon gave this high-handed answer to what he would have perceived as an impertinent question from his employee: "'I can swim across that river – I can snuff out that candle with a pistol-shot at the distance of twenty paces – and I have written a poem of which 14,000 copies were sold in one day.'"

Moore fails to record John's reply but we would imagine his sensitivity and literary ambition would have sent his feelings into a tail-spin. The question may have been intended as a light-hearted one, if, indeed, it was ever asked, but there is certainly no trace of a reference to this exchange in the diary or in any of Byron's letters. However, the aristocrat's response has a ring of truth and matches some of the terser barbs he would aim at his physician later in the year. By way of Byron myth-making, we have heard still further versions of this tale that have no doubt been extrapolated from Moore's comments; they have Byron replying , "'I can swim that river, snuff out that candle and give you a damn good thrashing.'"

We also crossed the Rhine from Rüdesheim to Bingen, albeit on a far less exotic vessel. At this point, the Rhine gorges drop to flatter land, yet from the Bingen banks the view stretches away to the distant terraced vineyards high above the river as the grape continues to be cultivated on impossibly steep ravine sides topped by castles in varying states of picturesque ruin. Our boat skirted the Mäuseturm, the curiously named Mouse Tower, which Polidori would have only seen in a shattered state; the legacy of a yet earlier French incursion. We saw a considerably smartened white and terracotta tower backed by the crumbling stone of Ehrenfels Castle on the opposite bank. In fact the Mäuseturm sits on its own island, a small channel separating it from Bingen.

The eighteenth and nineteenth-century British traveller was obsessed with the mysteries of the Rhine as evidenced by the many books produced during the period; for example, Joseph Snowe's *The Rhine: Legends, Traditions, History, from Cologne to Mainz* and Thomas Colley Grattan's *Lays and Legends of the Rhine*. The latter contains the story of the Mouse Tower, which first made its way into the English consciousness when it was included by Thomas Coryat, the Elizabethan eccentric wanderer and travel writer, in his wonderfully named book *Coryat's Crudities, hastily gobbled up in five moneths' travells*.

The original use of the tower was as a toll post for passing ships. If legend is to be believed, the Archbishop of Mainz, Hatto II, who was responsible for exacting payment, was a particularly cruel and ruthless ruler. Bowmen were stationed in the upper turret from where they could aim their arrows at non-contributors. Hatto also controlled the grain trade and would only release grain supplies at extortionate rates during a particularly bad famine. As peasants are wont to do in the face of tyranny, they revolted. To supposedly appease them, Hatto invited them all to an empty barn with the promise of grain.

Instead of feeding the poor, he locked them in and burnt them alive, commenting, according to the poet, Robert Southey, "'The merry mice! – how shrill they squeak!'" These words would prove fateful as the archbishop was set upon by a swarm of mice in his castle. By way of escape, he fled to his toll tower in the river hoping that the rodents could not swim. Unfortunately for him, although many died in the attempt, thousands of others crossed the channel and chewed through the wooden door, finally eating Hatto alive at the top of his turret. Southey graphically gives us this poetic finale:

> They have whetted their teeth against the stones,
> And now they pick the bishop's bones;
> They gnawed the flesh from every limb,
> For they were sent to do judgment on him!

Given that this poem was published in an anthology in 1800, it is entirely possible that Byron and Polidori knew of the story through these verses. Once a liberal in George Gordon's mould, Southey became more conservative in later life. Byron observed this political reversal and provides a mock dedication in *Don Juan*:

BOB SOUTHEY! You're a poet — Poet-laureate,
And representative of all the race;
Although 'tis true that you turn'd out a Tory at
Last, — yours has lately been a common case;
And now, my Epic Renegade! what are ye at?

These lines were not written at the time of their Rhine travels but it was Byron's ability to aim poisonous darts at the inflated egos of his peers that initially greatly appealed to the impressionable young doctor — that is, until the aristocrat's pointed wit was turned in Polidori's direction. And, if we believe Moore, this first took place on the waters of the great river.

Curiously, as far as legends are concerned, John pays scant regard to the Rhine's more mysterious iconography, Drachenfels being the exception. At Sankt Goar, where he must have had a splendid view of the Loreley Rock, the sirens make no entry in his diary; although he heard singing from the church, perhaps a distant echo of the maiden's song. Mark Twain covered much of the same ground in his 1880 book, *A Tramp Abroad*. He makes explicit reference to the Loreley story, which he calls "the people's favorite". Lore, a water nymph, used to sit on her rock, or 'ley', above Sankt Goarshausen. She lured boatmen with her haunting songs to their doom in a destructive rapid that ran between Sankt Goar and her outcrop.

As with most sagas involving a beautiful maiden, a young aristocrat fell head over heels in love with her and used to serenade her with his zither. Mooning around, he finally decided to sing to her from a boat on the river, thereby creating a turbulence in the waters that split his craft into pieces. Twain seems to think that the feckless youth deserved his fate, but ever since, the fairy nymph has never been seen but only heard. In typically self-deprecating and humorous fashion, Twain apologizes for his translation of the beautiful verses written by Heinrich Heine in 1823 that encapsulate the Loreley myth, from which we quote these lines:

I cannot divine what it meaneth,
This haunting nameless pain:

A tale of the bygone ages
Keeps brooding through my brain:
The faint air cools in the glooming,
And peaceful flows the Rhine,
The thirsty summits are drinking
The sunset's flooding wine . . .

Two years before Byron and Polidori, Mary Godwin – before she became a Shelley – travelled with Percy Bysshe and Claire Clairmont along the Rhine. This was not the journey that would take them to their destiny at the Villa Diodati but a previously aborted attempt at elopement. Confusion arises by the fact that in her *History of a six weeks' tour through a part of France, Switzerland, Germany and Holland*, she mentions Byron's lines written about Drachenfels in *Childe Harold*. Clearly, these were written by the poet after Mary's tour and the reference must have been added in at a later date.

Nonetheless, Mary's Rhine voyage was a piquant memory that would arise again in 1816 and we can see from her imagery that the river caught her creative imagination:

We were carried down by a dangerously rapid current, and saw on either side of us hills covered with vines and trees, craggy cliffs crowned by desolate towers, and wooded islands, where picturesque ruins peeped from behind the foliage, and cast the shadows of their forms on the troubled waters . . .

Vines, ruins, crags, sirens – it is difficult, almost impossible, to avoid Rhineland clichés. At least Polidori attempted some descriptions of the populace as well as the landscape, describing the cocked hats and buckles of the men pruning the vines. Modern-day viticulture inevitably has some mechanization but the imposing terrain limits the extent to which contemporary methods are relevant.

We passed estates that still maintain a hold on the entire production process from vine to bottle, even controlling both the marketing and sales. Due to the restrictive nature of the landscape, our riverside route was not so different from the carriage-rides of days past. Rather than Heine, we accompanied our own journey along the Rheinstrasse with the lilting lyrics of 'Lorelei' as sung by The Pogues, a testament to the enduring romance of the river's most famous and loved fable.

After Bingen, we know the Rhine takes on a more avuncular aspect, our doctor's "sublimity" of landscape replaced by gentler slopes. The next town of any significant size is Mainz, referred to by Polidori as Mayence. He was suitably impressed by its cosmopolitan atmosphere, describing it in these glowing terms: "Mayence a fine town, with a cathedral raised above it of red sandstone. Bavarians, Austrians, and Prussians, all in the town – belonging to all. The best town we have seen since Ghent."

The cathedral is something of a survivor having come through partial destruction by fire in the Middle Ages, constant additions and repairs, a lightning strike in 1767, Prussian bombardment at the end of that century and the Allied bombs of the Second World War. It remained untouched as over three-quarters of urban Mainz fell prey to air raids from the RAF and USAAF. Today, its scrubbed façade is best seen from Liebfrauenplatz where the view of the capitals of the portal facing the square is unhindered by surrounding buildings. If they have an Italianate feel, it is due to the fact they were sculpted by Lombard craftsmen as far back as the twelfth century.

Although the building is constructed in the aforementioned red sand-stone, the impression we received under a brilliant sun was one of a soft salmon pink edifice, carefully conserved and offset by the inspired idea of a municipal herb garden in front of the neighbouring Gutenberg Museum, pulsing waves of intense fragrance, nature's incense. The cloister is equally well-kept including a series of reliefs that were damaged by the Prussians shortly before Polidori visited. Of the marvels to be found in the interior – the Lady of Mainz in the Ketteler Chapel, the rococo choir stalls or the Gothic windows – John mentions little, instead focusing his attention on a bizarre monument high up in the East Choir.

A certain periwigged General Lahmberg is seen forcing open his own coffin in opposition to a skeletal figure with one bony hand on the General's escutcheon and the other firmly trying to slam the lid back down on the sarcophagus. We inspected the curious ensemble as closely as distance would allow noting the more reassuring presence of an angel at his feet and the accoutrements of his profession supporting the structure. Try as we might, we could not see the inscription Polidori translated, "'I am here'", a peculiar statement that gives the whole ensemble a final Gothic flourish. For the physician who would subsequently write *The Vampyre*, this vision of an aristocrat rising from the dead must have lurked in the recesses of his mind.

Our mention of a Gutenberg Museum indicates Mainz's place in the history of letters. It was from a house on the corner of Christofsstrasse that Henne Gensfleisch zur Laden set up his printing press. Better known to history as Johannes Gutenberg, he was the originator of mechanical movable type, an invention that revolutionized the production of books in the fifteenth century. Polidori claimed that he was unable to see this building as it had been destroyed by the French, although he may have been referring to one of several edifices associated with the printer in his home town. Certainly, the house saw many changes and was completely obliterated in the Second World War, being replaced by a pharmacy.

Part of the Hof zum Humbrecht still stands where Gutenberg and his partner Fust established another press that would produce the Gutenberg Bible. The remaining white stair tower is visible from Am Brand, wedged between shops and offices, a piece of lead type lodged between the buttons of a Windows keyboard. Two copies of the eponymous bible are on display in the Museum, but the city's most prominent monument to its famous son is the bronze statue opposite the Staatstheater. It was erected in 1837 thanks to subscriptions collected from many countries in Europe. The sculptor was the feted Dane, Bertel Thorvaldsen, who twenty years earlier had completed a bust of Lord Byron.

Byron liked the result but could not resist a customary drop of acid when referring to the sculpture in a letter dated 1821: "A picture is a different matter – everybody sits for a picture: but a bust looks like putting up pretensions to permanency, and smacks of a hankering for public fame rather than private remembrance." Thorvaldsen, however, recalled Byron as a difficult sitter who tried to manipulate his pose and expression to fit the public view of him as the melancholic romantic poet. Not to be compromised, the Dane portrayed him in a work that many have claimed to be the aristocrat's greatest likeness. The original can be seen in the Thorvaldsen Museum in Copenhagen.

Before heading to Mannheim, we could not resist a small detour to a place on the map that demanded our attention. Neither of our two nineteenth-century travelling companions mentioned the location in diaries or letters but many have claimed it had a significant effect on the Shelleys two years previously. Burg Frankenstein lies fourteen kilometres from Darmstadt and is a fifty-minute drive from Mainz. The Bergstrasse, amply signposted from the main road, spirals upwards from the plain. The narrow two-lane tarmacked road mirrors the coach tracks of old, eventually reaching the ruin sitting on a wooded hilltop.

Research tells us that the castle made its first written appearance in a 1252 charter, thereafter being the residence of the Frankenstein family for the next 400 years. It was in 1662 that the Frankensteins sold it to the Landgrave of Hessen-Darmstadt, but not before they had expanded the buildings to incorporate an estate. The drive to the summit on a summer's day, aided by the mesmeric road, is a dream-like experience, the sun-split foliage providing tantalizing glimpses of the crumbling outer walls of the fortress. The approach to the western gate brings the full edifice into view with its two towers, crenelated walls and Gothic appearance. The towers seem to belong to separate dwellings, an impression borne out by the fact that they were inhabited by different branches of the family after a dispute.

The name clearly resonates with Mary Shelley's eponymous creation but why this choice for her protagonist's surname? Scholars and historians disagree and it is by no means clear that the Shelleys actually visited the castle in 1814. Radu Florescu, in his excellent book *In Search of Frankenstein*, makes a convincing case for Mary's awareness of the legends that surround the fortress. The aborted 1814 elopement saw the couple and Claire Clairmont return home via the Rhine and Florescu makes the point that the river is only some fourteen kilometres away, as the crow flies, although this depends on the point at which you leave the river. He quotes from Mary's journal for 2 September where there is a three hour period unaccounted for that she spent with Shelley. Claire's diary, although somewhat different, has the trio mooring overnight near Gernsheim, the closest Rhine port. Reading between the lines, Florescu is giving them sufficient time to have reached the castle walls.

In many ways, it is irrelevant whether the trio trod the actual footpaths of the Frankenstein family as it is most likely that they would have heard or read about the myths and legends. Today, a leaflet available to visitors is clearly trying to distance itself from the book and instead shine a spotlight on the family's stories:

> Castle Frankenstein is often described as a mysterious place. But there aren't any connections to Mary Shelley's novel "Frankenstein". In 1814, the English author had been on a boat trip on the river Rhine. She had a break for a couple of hours in Gernsheim/Rhine — but in the middle of the night. As Gernsheim is approximately 15 miles (linear distance) far from Castle Frankenstein you can hardly see the castle, even by day! However, Castle Frankenstein is rich in authentic legends.

We feel this is missing the point, as it is precisely these legends that could have hovered in Mary Shelley's consciousness and contributed to the many influences behind her novel. The Frankenstein name can be translated as the 'stone' or 'fortress of the Franks' and given the proximity to France, there are many names that have this prefix. A certain Arbogast was the originator of the dynasty and a knight of Cologne. Problems arose for the family, according to Florescu, when they retained their Catholicism in the face of the ruling Protestants of Hesse who put a curse on these recalcitrant underlings.

In the castle, there is a small chapel, standing alone, that contains two poignant effigies of Hans von Frankenstein and his wife Irmel von Cleen. She, veiled and kneeling, holds a prayer book; he, also kneeling and in armour, clasps his hands in prayer. Pilgrim shells form the niches above their heads. Supposedly, their violent deaths at a young age were a product of the curse that also saw others in the family die prematurely.

An even stranger story is that of Lord Georg. He was a knight who was beseeched by the local peasantry to combat the "Scheusslicher

Lindwurm" – a serpent or dragon-like creature that had been hiding out in the local well. Donning his full armour, Georg strode forth and dispatched the beast but, in its death throes, it managed to wrap a poisonous tale around the knight's leg and pierce his skin through a gap in the armour. Lord Georg's tomb in nearby Nieder-Beerbach shows him standing on the dragon with the creature's lethal tale entwined around his leg. A version of the story was adapted by the Brothers Grimm.

The most relevant history to the evolution of *Frankenstein*, the book, is that of the alchemist Johann Konrad Dippel. Although not a member of the family by birth, he grew up at the castle as a war refugee in the late seventeenth century and styled himself whilst at university "Franckensteina", implying he was of the estate. He was a solitary savant who soon distinguished himself in the fields of chemistry and alchemical study. Time spent first at Giessen University and then at Strasbourg saw him develop his skills but he left the latter university under a cloud and returned home to Darmstadt where he received the patronage of Count Ernst Ludwig of Hesse. Dippel now had the money to pursue alchemy, specifically the transformation of base metals into gold.

At the beginning of the eighteenth century, he claimed that he had found the philosopher's stone and could produce gold. Florescu says that legend has Dippel using his gains to buy an estate near the Bergstrasse, thereby breaking the tradition that alchemists never use their created wealth for personal advantage. By way of punishment, he lost his secret when the jar containing the legendary stone broke. Moving to Berlin, Dippel turned his attention to distilled animal blood and bones which, when crushed and condensed, became his famous oil. A by-product of these experiments was the artists' substance known as Prussian Blue.

Swedish scientist and philosopher, Emanuel Swedenborg, was Dippel's disciple and then collaborator who eventually went on to denounce him as a "most vile devil ... who attempted wicked things". Further rumours abounded as regards the alchemist's experimentation with cadavers; his writings do mention the transference of souls from one body to another. With the promise of a chemical secret, Dippel tried to purchase Castle Frankenstein but was refused by the Landgrave. The myth perpetuated by many is that he wanted to create a clandestine laboratory in the ruin.

By way of an aside, the Prussian Blue that Dippel created was later cut with sulphuric acid to create prussic acid – a substance that would have a very substantial impact on John Polidori. If the alchemist's chemical solutions have lasted, so have the legends surrounding Castle Frankenstein. Returning once again to Radu Florescu's well-researched book, the author was warned off an overnight stay in the castle's inn in the early 1970s when a local soothsayer told him to depart before the chapel bell struck midnight.

We too decided to avoid the bewitching hour, retracing out steps back down the Bergstrasse to pick up the Byron-Polidori trail at Zwingenberg on the way to Mannheim. In his journal, the doctor tells us that he was taken ill with a fever along this route. Consequently, little appears with reference to these towns. It meant, however, that he had the time to devote more detailed paragraphs to his state of health whilst recuperating in Karlsruhe. He took ipecac and opium to combat his symptoms, followed by magnesia and lemon acid – a combination that to modern ears is enough to make anyone feel ill.

Generally speaking, John Polidori has suffered at the hands of novel-ists and film makers intent on fictionalizing the spring and summer of 1816. Ken Russell in *Gothic* has the physician as a snivelling older man in the guise of the splendid but miscast Timothy Spall. The French writer, Emmanuel Carrère, starts his book, *Gothic Romance*, with Polidori as an opium addict living in a squat with a prostitute, whilst Benjamin Markovits in *Imposture* actually conjures up a Polidori who goes to the extreme of impersonating Byron. In Paul West's racy *Lord Byron's Doctor*, closely following the actual journal, West fictionalizes John's fragile state at this point in the journey:

> To Carlsruhe I clattered through a grove of Scotch firs, only to enter the (non-Scotch) inn reeling and perspiring, jelly in the knees and needles in the eyes. Heal thyself, I said aloud in bed, and dosed myself with ipecac, *Cephaelis ipecacuanha*, with 15 grains of opium. There followed vertigo, headache, and a ten-

dency to syncope, none of these helped by magnesia and lemon acid. I cheered but felt worse, in some phase of my dementia imagining I saw a long shelf with my life's works (books) all arranged with titles in alphabetical order, but I could see only the first letters of these titles.

The ipecac referred to above was known in Europe as far back as Nicholas Culpeper's 1653 *Complete Herbal & English Physician*. It is an emetic derived from the *Rubiaceae* plant family and commonly found in Brazil, hence the name quoted by West above. This, together with the laxative properties of magnesium citrate, suggests that the doctor was keen to flush his system as soon as nature would allow.

Foolishly, he decided to accompany Byron on a carriage ride around Karlsruhe, commenting on the white stucco of the houses and the pain it caused his eyes. With a novelist's flourish, West has Polidori experiencing burning sensations from the glare of the brilliant paint, thus worsening an already crippling headache. He came to the Karlsruher Schloss, the only building of note he mentions in the city, which is understandable given his feverish state. The palace was constructed in the early part of the eighteenth century, the final stone being placed in 1715. The Second World War did its best to reduce the palace to rubble but it was swiftly rebuilt and we saw it in its reconstructed splendour, now the site of the Badisches Landesmuseum; the wings of its imposing façade still stretched out in formal welcome.

Polidori was much less inclined to saunter in the gardens, then as now, laid out in the English country-house style. He returned home to the inn, and unwisely took some advice to eat stewed apples with yet more lemon acid. It is at this point in the relationship between Byron and his physician that we glimpse a further insight into the strange dynamic between these two ill-suited characters. Milord was a notably tetchy character when his plans were offset or delayed by circumstances unforeseen and it is not inconceivable that John's sickness had sent him into an ill humour. After a few hours rest, the doctor was again attempting to go out for a gentle stroll when Byron stopped him, snatched the silver-plated candlestick he was holding and tried to replace it with a brass one when Polidori fainted. The servants came running to his aid and he tells us that he took four (unspecified) pills to restore a degree of equilibrium. As he finally gathered enough strength to take some air, Byron yet again insisted the servants attending John have the brass stick instead of the plate one.

On the surface, this appears to be an insignificant incident but the implications for the pair were more profound. In Polidori's hour of need, a frustrated Byron asserted his hierarchical status as the aristocrat entitled to the very best and anyone beneath him, unwell or not, had to be content with less. By stamping his authority on the employee doctor, he was, in effect, stamping on the ego of a man who felt he was the intellectual equal of Byron – these were not mere candlesticks but symbols of more psychological warfare to come.

Fortunately, his master's haughty demeanour was not mirrored by other visitors who came to seek out the stricken doctor. After a period of purging, Polidori felt "better on the whole, though weak" and was happy to receive Sir C Hunter, an English notable whom we have been unable to track down in the annals of history. Seemingly, he was well-enough acquainted to be a friend of the Grand Duke of Baden and regaled anyone who would listen with "long sermons" about rheumatism and the appropriate routes to take into Switzerland. By way of help, he sent to Polidori the far more useful *Guide du Voyagers en les pays del'Europe*; although we suspect this was a bid to obtain some hand-written poems from Byron in exchange.

The only guide that we have been able to uncover that corresponds to the given title and the possible routes the pair would be taking is Reichard's 1805 *Guide des Voyageurs en Europe* which certainly covers France, Belgium, the German states, Switzerland and Italy. Whatever the details of the exact publication, no doubt the pages were well-thumbed when Polidori moved on towards the Swiss border and beyond, as he makes explicit reference to the guide in future diary entries.

Their pace of travel now begins to pick up speed; Offenberg and its "woods with mists" rapidly disappeared into the distance as the entourage headed for Krolzingen – a destination that caused us some head-scratching until we established he had been referring to Bad Krozingen, a town that, as the name suggests, was renowned for its spas. Polidori's sights, however, were firmly set on the mountains: "Left

Krolzingen: got to a hill. Fine view thence: the Alps, the Rhine, the Jura mountains, and a fine plain before us – fine country. Crossed the Rhine, and were in Switzerland." The Shelleys and Claire Clairmont would be lying in wait for them in Geneva.

CHAPTER FOUR

Switzerland
The Summer of Creation

The Rhine forms a natural border between the three countries that meet just to the north of Basle. A few metres beyond Westquaistrasse, the frontiers intersect in the middle of the river, with France to the west, Germany to the east and Switzerland to the south-east. There is no bridge at this point and there was only one available, the Mittlere Rheinbrücke, until 1879. This structure was rebuilt in 1905, but the original span dates back to the thirteenth century and was the first bridge to be constructed over the Rhine.

On 19 May 1816, Polidori stood on this prosaically titled Middle Rhine Bridge and contemplated the scene: "The town upon unequal ground – some parts very high, and some low; the greater part very narrow streets." Walk along Schafgässlein, at right angles to the Rheingasse, and it is still possible to glimpse a hint of the Basle that John has conjured for us. The opposite bank is home to the majority of the city's museums, including the Fine Arts Museum in St Alban-Graben, which now houses the works that Polidori details in his diary entry two days later.

He is very dismissive of a panorama depicting the town of Thun on the shores of the lake bearing the same name. A quick perusal of the museum's collection uncovers three panoramas, all painted by Marquard Fidel Dominikus Wocher, but none of them quite reflect our doctor's criticism that the picture was "crowded foolishly with people, and too small". In fact, the trio are completely devoid of the human figure. Polidori says that the panorama, which forms a complete circle, was kept in a gallery that the artist had created. In 1814, Wocher did actually open his own display space in Sternengasse. The painting has

The Villa Diodati, Cologny, A. Edwards

Plaque commemorating Byron on the wall of the Villa Diodati, Cologny, S. Edwards

Stone commemorating the 100 year anniversary of Byron's death, Le Pré Byron, Cologny, S. Edwards

View of the castle of Chillon, Jan Gerard Waldorp, after Michel Vincent Brandoin, 1792, Rijksmuseum

now been moved to the town it portrays. The local art museum's website shows the canvas above a contemporary photograph with 200 years separating the images. Remarkably little appears to have changed in the centre of the town.

The old master that everyone associates with Basle is Holbein and Polidori was no different in trying to seek out his works. He was to be disappointed when he found that much of the artist's output had been dispersed. In 1515, Hans Holbein the Younger was apprenticed to Hans Herbster, then the city's leading painter, and was present during an explosion in book publishing, which saw him illustrate the title page of Martin Luther's Bible for the publisher Johann Froben. Holbein's portrait of Froben hangs in the Fine Arts Museum having been acquired for the city in 1811.

John lamented the destruction of the artist's supposed illustrations of *The Dance of Death* on a mural, but was right in thinking that the work was not actually Holbein's, attributing it instead to "his restorer". Polidori would have been better advised to search the antiquarian book sellers' establishments as Holbein was the first to produce the macabre dance in book format. A 1549 edition shows an armoured knight wielding a sword whilst being pierced in the side by the lance of a skeletal figure representing Death. The knight contorts in agony and defiance as the sands of time at their feet swiftly run out. John's bedtime reading was less ghoulish, but equally fantastical. As the party left Basle and headed south via a stop at a local hostelry, Polidori took the *Arabian Nights* to bed.

It seems that the doctor had overpaid the coachmen for their drink money by quite some margin according to the figures recommended by the *Guide du Voyageur*; consequently progress was slow. Byron, how-ever, made no attempt at reprimanding his largesse and this part of the journey seems to have passed with little incident. They travelled through Soleure which is more commonly referred to by its Swiss German name of Solothurn. By now, we are familiar with Polidori's habit of passing comment on the local women, but at least the follow-ing description has an ethnographical aspect as well as a lascivious one: "women ornamented strangely – amazingly short petticoats, not below the knee, with black crape rays round their heads that make them look very spidery".

His attention to regional costume would come in handy years later when he was asked to provide the text for Richard Bridgens' illustrations in the book *Costumes of Italy, Switzerland and France*. This is now a rare volume and we only managed to view a copy in the British Library. The etched and tinted drawings are quaintly evocative and the well-written text is reminiscent of the Victorian explorer matter-of-factly expounding on the peoples in some far flung region of Asia. Here we have an example of Polidori's commentary on the costume of Mount Cenis in the neighbouring French Alps:

> Experience is the guide of everything: we have seen that the lower orders seldom vary in their dress from generation to generation. When they have once found out the best defence against the effects of the climate, in which they are born, they keep to it, only ornamenting or varying those parts, which are not of importance against the weather.
>
> Amongst the Alps, the peasant protects himself against the cold; in the marshes against the damp; and on the plain against the heat. The females of Mount Cenis are almost mattressed round, and their broad brims form a constant umbrella.

The cover of the book is a roundel encompassing the title, which is surrounded by all manner of folkloric items from a pitcher and basket to a fork and mattock. Richard Bridgens' name is proudly displayed underneath the title of the work. Ever the forgotten man, there is no mention of the wordsmith, John William Polidori. Like a ghost, his unattributed words have come down to us on these pages and leafing through this 1821 volume left us with a profound sense of melancholy. We imagined Polidori hard at work on the text for which he knew he would receive no credit and little financial reward. The ultimate irony, though, and a ray of light, is to be found in the library's catalogue entry, *"Sketches Illustrative of the Manners and Costumes of France, Switzerland, and Italy*, by John William Polidori. [Plates, with accompanying text.]". Bridgens is listed as a mere afterthought.

From Solothurn, the party made the briefest of stops in Berne where they ate and then caught their first glimpse of Morat (Murten) where they would stay the night. Polidori mentions the Crown Inn which still exists and has been merged with the neighbouring Murtenhof to form the Hotel Murtenhof and Krone in Rathausgasse. This is the heart of the medieval old town, where the arcaded streets are dotted with rounded watchtowers, capped with conical terracotta tiling. To add to the almost too perfect Swissness of it all, Lake Murten offers a panorama of compact beauty backed by the vineyards of the Vully region where the chasselas grape is grown.

Murten is on a linguistic boundary between French and German speaking Switzerland and historically has been the scene of conflict. In 1476, it was the battleground for the armies of the Duke of Burgundy, Charles the Bold, and the Swiss Confederation. Rattled by previous defeat, Charles had regrouped his straggling troops and drove them from Lausanne to the Murtensee with the intention of taking the town. The Burgundians laid siege to the settlement's fortifications. Meanwhile, a Confederate relief force was on its way.

The Swiss rained down on the interlopers and pinned them against the lake. With nowhere to go, the Burgundians were routed. Charles tried, in vain, to use his last line of defence – his English archers – but their leader was killed by a Swiss soldier before they could unleash their arrows. Supposedly, the Duke of Somerset was the commander who had been struck down but given that he had died five years before this battle, it is highly unlikely.

Time crystallizes certain events but for the twenty-first century Anglo-Saxon, time has eroded these memories. Not so for Byron and Polidori who went in search of the chapel remains that had displayed the Burgundian soldiers' bones. An ossuary was built in 1485 to house the thousands of bones from the defeated army. In 1797, the region of Vaud declared its independence and was occupied by the French. Amongst the French troops, there were many Burgundians keen to wipe from history the massive defeat of their forebears; therefore, they set about trying to burn down the ossuary. This first attempt at destruction failed as did their second salvo with gunpowder. Finally, the building was levelled to the ground.

It was in this state that Byron and his doctor saw what was left of the memorial. John tells us:

Their bones, of which we took pieces, are now very few; once they formed a mighty heap in the chapel, but both were destroyed by the Burgundian division when in Switzerland, and a tree of liberty was planted over it, which yet flourishes in all its verdure – the liberty has flown from the planters' grasp.

Lord Byron was, as always, less descriptive of the scene, but more piquant in his black humour. He wrote to Hobhouse that he had "brought away the leg and wing of a Burgundian". Ever a champion of the freedom-fighter, the poet felt inspired enough by the original Swiss counter-attack against the rather rash Charles of Burgundy to include the battlefield in Canto III of *Childe Harold*:

But ere these matchless heights I dare to scan,
There is a spot should not bpass'd in vain, –
Morat! the proud, the patriot field! where man
May gaze on ghastly trophies of the slain,
Nor blush for those who conquer'd on that plain;
Here Burgundy bequeath'd his tombless host,
A bony heap, through ages to remain,
Themselves their monument; – the Stygian coast
Unsepulchred they roam'd, and shrieked each wandering ghost.

While Waterloo with Cannae carnage vies,
Morat and Marathon twin names shall stand;
They were true Glory's stainless victories,
Won by the unambitious heart and hand
Of a proud, brotherly, and civic band,
All unbought champions in no princely cause
Of vice-entail'd Corruption; they no land
Doom'd to bewail the blasphemy of laws
Making kings' rights divine, by some Draconian clause.

Back in the Crown for supper, Polidori was button-holed by the innkeeper who was slightly the worse for wear. Sadly, John does not elaborate on the conversation but simply says that he "being a little tipsy, and thinking every Englishman (being a philosophe) must be a philosophe like himself, favoured us with some of his infidel notions". The modern Swiss proprietor would not dream of inflicting anything remotely approaching "infidel notions" upon a paying guest, even less be caught with a hand on the bottle whilst on duty.

The avalanche of history did not stop with Murten, but continued in the neighbouring town of Avenches, once Aventicum, the Roman capital of Helvetia. At the end of the Rue Centrale are the remains of the amphitheatre; unlike sunnier climes, its banks of stone steps are covered in grass, where the audience would once have sat. It has a homely feel, much like a provincial theatre, belying the monstrous events that took place within its confines. John mentions the structure in his diary and also talks of the strewn artefacts that were only just coming to light, such as the mosaic pavement that could be discerned when the summer grass thinned, a head of Apollo and "plinths, capitals, and shafts, heaped promiscuously".

In an age before systematic archaeology, Polidori is nonetheless scathing of the good burghers of Avenches for the lack of care with regard to their past: "The town is shamefully negligent of the antiquities of their fathers, for there is another more beautiful and perfect mosaic pavement discovered, but which they have allowed the proprietor to cover again with mould rather than buy it." This common disregard, so prevalent in the early nineteenth century, has been more than rectified and the Musée Romain, housed in the amphitheatre's tower, now contains many of the promiscuously strewn articles viewed by the doctor.

Aventicum also makes an appearance in *Childe Harold* by way of Julia Alpinula, a young priestess who died whilst trying to save her condemned father. Our duo went in search of an inscription in a local church that related to Julia but to no avail. Of particular interest to Polidori was another Latin inscription dedicated to the followers of Hypocrates. The museum now safely keeps the limestone altar with the engraved writing that he copied in his notebook. Quintus Postumius Hyginus and Postumius Hermes lauded the medical profession at their own expense with the creation of the altar. If only Byron had thought of his doctor in the same reverential terms. In all honesty, he probably had more faith in the pseudo-physicians who ministered to Hyginus and Hermes.

The pastoral classicism of Aventicum even had John conjuring a Sicilian scene straight from the poetry of Theocritus as the whole entourage moved on to Payerne. A young shepherd, who undoubtedly had more in common with Peter the Goat-herder, suddenly became a bucolic Grecian figure "in the antique style". The shepherd was wandering through the rolling landscape that surrounds the Murtensee, which is relatively flat for Switzerland. However, the tempting horizons had the party debating "whether clouds were mountains, or mountains clouds".

They skirted Lac Neuchatel and passed through Moudon, which Polidori deemed "dirty", an adjective that could seldom be ascribed to Swiss settlements these days, but was surprisingly apt in the nineteenth century. The road they followed took them into the landward side of Lausanne which remains true for the contemporary traveller, although they would not have had to contend with the functional suburbs dotted with industrial estates and retail parks.

Lausanne offered them their first view of Lake Geneva which the doctor addresses by its correct local name, Léman. He is less taken by the spectacle than one would have imagined, especially as Byron stored it in his poetic imagination for later use in Childe Harold: "Lake Leman woos me with its crystal face, / The mirror where the stars and mountains view / The stillness of their aspect in each trace . . . " John admitted that "We went along the lake, that a little disappointed me as it does not seem so broad as it really is . . . " To give him his due, we also concluded that Lausanne does not offer the viewer the lake's best aspect.

More precisely, the port area is the district of Ouchy, a haven for the yachting fraternity which gives an air of quiet extravagance to the lakeside. The Quai d'Ouchy is also home to the Musée Olympique, commemorating the modern Olympic movement. Even in Byron's day, the port was beginning to develop facilities for the wealthy tourist. The poet would leave his footprint in the town along with Percy Shelley during a weather-enforced stay but, for the time being, he and the doctor were just passing through *en route* to Geneva.

As their coach rattled along the water's edge, Polidori became very aware that he was travelling in the wake of some illustrious names –

"Buonaparte, Joseph, Bonnet, Necker, Staël, Voltaire, Rousseau, all have their villas (except Rousseau). Genthoud, Ferney, Coppet, are close to the road." Voltaire and Rousseau were always going to appeal to the new generation of liberal Romantics with their anti-establishment attitudes and free-thinking. The French enlightenment writer, Voltaire, once exiled in Britain, had come to rest in the town of Ferney which now appends his name to their signs. After annoying the Calvinist Genevans, he decamped to the French side of the border in 1758 and bought a large estate, where he received many an English visitor with a mixture of curiosity and irritation.

We also chose to decamp to the French side and stayed in Ferney-Voltaire. Although drawn by the town's eminent former resident, our true motive was less worthy; the hotel prices in Ferney were but a fraction of their extortionate Swiss counterparts. Residents of Geneva are also well-aware of the difference in the cost of living, judging by the quantity of Swiss number-plates in Ferney's Carrefour carpark. The town is remarkably close to central Geneva and the border sweeps alongside the city's airport runway. Owing to the Schengen Accord between the European Union and Switzerland, crossing the frontier is no more problematic than driving between Belgium and Germany. Mercifully, the backroads past the deserted border posts are not subject to the 50 Euro toll you have to pay when crossing into Switzerland at the Basle motorway junction.

Heading towards the lake along the Route de Ferney, the first Genevan suburb that comes into view is Sécheron, now linked to the centre by a continuous ribbon of development. Byron and Polidori saw it in a far more rural state, the settlement being firmly outside the city gates. On 25 May, they arrived at the doors of the Hotel d'Angleterre, where an exhausted Byron was so tired he jotted down his age in the guestbook as "one hundred".

The hotel, run by a Monsieur Dejean, was already well-known to English visitors, something that must have prompted Byron to look for alternative accommodation as soon as possible. The hotel, which is no longer in operation, was situated in what is now known as the Parc Moynier. A new establishment, built in 1872, carries the same name and is a short distance away on the Quai du Mont-Blanc.

Already waiting at the hotel were Percy Bysshe Shelley, Mary Godwin (his future wife) and her step-sister, Claire Clairmont. Claire had already pestered Byron into an affair that had started shortly before the aristocrat left England. Like a star-struck groupie, she had pursued her prey, ignoring the lascivious rumours about the poet circulating London at the time. Percy Shelley's excellent biographer, Richard Holmes, tells us that, even though it was Claire's plan to head for Geneva in search of Byron, Shelley was more than happy to agree to the idea as he saw it as the perfect opportunity to meet a like-minded soul. Mary, however, was rather more limited in her understanding of the situation's complexity.

Shelley and his female companions took rooms on the upper floor of the d'Angleterre with views over the water and out towards the Alps. Confining themselves to the hotel, its gardens and the lake, the little group spent their time reading Italian and Latin during the day and boating in the evening, languidly drifting across the lake's clear surface. They had to wait ten days for Byron to appear. The commotion of his arrival was obvious to all and it was not long before Claire passed him a covert note requesting an assignation using Shelley as the go-between. Typically, Byron ignored the missive causing Claire much distress.

A further plea, complaining of his "marked indifference" went unacknowledged, forcing her to engineer a supposedly chance encounter when she spotted Byron and Polidori coming in to land from a boating excursion. John recalls the meeting in his diary in the following interesting extract:

> Home, and looked at the accounts: bad temper on my side. Went into a boat, rowed across to Diodati; cannot have it for three years; English family. Crossed again; I went; LB back. Getting out LB met M Wollstonecraft Godwin, her sister, and Percy Shelley. I got into the boat into the middle of Leman Lake, and there lay my length, letting the boat go its way.

As Polidori drifted aimlessly, gazing at the scudding clouds, Byron was inviting Shelley to dine that evening. The doctor returned to find that he, too, was to make up the numbers at the dinner party. It seems that the two poets were somewhat formal on their first meeting, and no doubt Shelley was in awe of his more famous counterpart. Polidori tells us as much when he writes: "PS, the author of *Queen Mab*, came; bashful, shy, consumptive; twenty-six; separated from his wife; keeps the two daughters of Godwin, who practise his theories; one LB's."

This staccato litany of opaque information needs some explanation. Firstly, it is unclear whether Polidori actually thought that Shelley was a tuberculosis sufferer or that he was using the term "consumptive" to give a general description of Shelley's slight build and pale countenance; we favour the latter. John had also added three years to Percy's age. However, the most revealing aspect of the comment is that which refers to the daughters of Godwin who "practise his theories". Claire was not William Godwin's daughter but became part of the family when her mother married him. He was an advocate of women's rights and took a liberal view with regard to the sexual mores of the time, but was not able to apply these when Shelley ran off with his daughter, Mary.

Shelley was an advocate of free love. He had left his wife, Harriet, to take up with Mary and had even encouraged her to experiment with his best friend, Thomas Hogg. Polidori suggests that Shelley was also in a relationship with Claire, a tantalizing assertion that even the best of biographers have never been able to pin down. Richard Holmes strongly hints that during the many months the three spent together, Percy would have slept with Claire. Their relationship was close enough for Mary to often wish for "*absentia Clariae*". Polidori was astute, though, in noticing Claire and Byron. By 27 May, it was clear to the doctor that there was a romantic entanglement between his employer and Mary's step-sister.

Byron was uncomfortable with being the focus of attention for the gawping guests at the hotel. It took him just one day to visit potential houses to rent. As we have already seen, Polidori was distressed to find that the Villa Diodati at Cologny, across the lake from Sécheron, had already been booked for three years. The poet engaged a Swiss banker, Charles Hentsch, to try and negotiate the possibility of a stay at the villa. The party had no alternative but to wait at Sécheron for a decision to be made.

Polidori was not slow in filling his time – partly with house-hunting missions for his employer and partly in making new acquaintances. It was the first time since leaving Dover that John and Byron had the opportunity and space to follow different paths for an extended period. With the arrival of Shelley, Byron had a new focus which would ultimately place a great strain on the already tenuous relationship between the doctor and the poet. John headed into Geneva and found himself in the company of fellow medics.

In 1816, Geneva had a population of approximately 30,000 which, although relatively small, belies its impact on European affairs. It had become a beacon for stolid Protestantism in the mould of John Calvin, the French theologian who adopted the city and set up its university in 1559. Perversely, it was also starting to be known as a refuge for the politically dispossessed of other nations. As the century progressed, it would become a haven for Russian émigrés with a grudge against the tsarist regime.

The medieval heart of Geneva would have been much more apparent to Polidori than it is today, with its curious mixture of French and Germanic influences. Modern development has enfolded the old town, centred on the Cathedral of Saint Pierre to the south of the river Rhône, which dissects the city. Wandering the narrow streets, we were already anticipating the solid, cleanly scrubbed order that surrounded us. The buildings offer a sense of security in their steadfast immutability. Perhaps we had imbued our concept of Genevan architecture with preconceived notions derived from the city's austere religiosity; although such ascetic spirituality screams its presence under the Gothic arches of the cathedral.

In one of John's many trips from Sécheron to the centre of town, he even found the city gates firmly shut for the simple expediency of a church service. He went in search of Pellegrino Rossi whom he had met at a soiree hosted by Madame Einard, having previously been in the company of a Dr de Roche. Rossi was an Italian expatriate who had been exiled for his political opinions and Polidori felt an instant affinity with him. On their first meeting, they discussed the respective merits of Dante and Ariosto. By way of macho paternalistic advice, Rossi told John that the women of Geneva were "amazingly chaste"; an assertion that John must have already assumed.

As soon as his new acquaintances realized that he was Byron's doctor, they badgered him for information about the now notorious aristocrat. Invitations flooded in, but always with the hope that Lord Byron would deign to make an appearance. Professor Pictet of the Geneva Observatory requested their attendance whilst Dr Odier opened the doors of his musical society. Polidori found that he shared a common interest in somnambulism with Odier and at last found himself respected for his specialist knowledge on an esoteric subject. The Swiss medic put his library at John's disposal and passed on many of his treaties on the matter.

In contrast to the friends he was making in these Swiss academic circles, Polidori and Byron were increasingly testing each other's patience. Another escape from the confines of the hotel took the pair across the lake with Shelley. John notes that during this trip Byron "quarrelled with me". The sketchy outline Polidori gives us has been embellished by others.

Thomas Moore is the traditional source used to flesh out the details. He states that John had sarcastically claimed to be happy after having accidentally hit Byron on the knee with an oar. In Moore's words, his lordship was aghast at hearing the doctor's delight in his pain and reports him as saying: "'It was with some difficulty that I refrained from throwing you into the water; and but for Mrs Shelley's presence, I should probably have done some such rash thing.'" The problem with conflating John's three words with Moore's account is that Mary was not in the boat at the time. It seems that John was always the easy target for biographers.

Byron was also becoming increasingly irritated by his fellow coun-trymen swarming to Switzerland and found the city lousy with English. Their loose tongues and gossipy manner gave rise to the most outlandish of rumours. Somehow, these reports of fake news made their way back to Britain, reportedly prompting Byron's arch enemy, Robert Southey, to say that the poet was in a "League of Incest" with Claire and Mary.

Polidori gives a memorable description in his diary, dated 5 June, of the English in Geneva. He was at Dr Odier's and conversing with some of the Genevan *beau monde* when he noticed this little vignette: "Quantities of English; speaking amongst themselves, arms by their sides, mouths open and eyes glowing; might as well make a tour of the Isle of Dogs." This makes uncomfortable reading as it is undoubtedly still true of some middle Englanders who dare to travel abroad. At the other end of the spectrum, the inhibited English person throws all caution to the wind after several garish cocktails, collapsing in the street or throwing up in an Ibizan gutter.

Whilst John was observing the English, Shelley, Mary and Claire had found a property to rent for the summer. The Maison Chapuis was a stone's throw from Byron's thwarted Villa Diodati and situated on Montalègre overlooking the lake near Cologny. Polidori had accompanied the Shelleys, rowing across the lake on a fact-finding trip. Sadly, the Maison no longer exists but old black and white photographs show an almost cube-like residence, its sloping tiled roof charmingly pierced through with chimney pots. It was close enough to the lake to have its own small harbour where Shelley, and subsequently Byron, would anchor their boats.

Radu Florescu, the author of *In Search of Frankenstein*, was able to track down descendants of the last person to own Chapuis and discovered that the building was pulled down in 1883, only to be reconstructed, brick by brick, at Pointe de la Bise in neighbouring Collonges. Try as we might, we could find nothing that resembled the structure. Florescu also tells us that there was a stable next to the Cologny house which has now been turned into a dwelling. In the 1970s, when he visited the area, he spoke to one of the owners who reported that an English tenant had complained of a ghost. Apparently, steps had been heard during the night on the stairs between the first and second floors. Reassuringly, the author was informed that the spectre was a kindly, lyrical figure, inferring that the ghost belonged to Percy Bysshe Shelley.

Despite the blossoming friendship between Shelley and Byron, Polidori was, at this point, still able to cultivate a relationship with Percy and Mary. In another of his insightful and pithy diary entries, he analyses the path that led Shelley to Switzerland:

Gone through much misery, thinking he was dying; married a girl for the mere sake of letting her have the jointure that would accrue to her; recovered; found he could not agree; separated; paid Godwin's debts, and seduced his daughter; then wondered that he would not see him. The sister left the father to go with the other. Got a child. All clever, and no meretricious appearance. He is very clever: the more I read his *Queen Mab*, the more beauties I find. Published at fourteen a novel; got £30 for it; by his second work £100.

A very young Percy, freshly expelled from Oxford for his atheism, did indeed marry Harriet Westbrook in a bid to free her from an unhappy life and to provide her with an inheritance. The horrible end to this tragic tale would not be long in coming. Just seven months after Polidori committed these words to paper, Harriet would be found dead in the Serpentine in London's Hyde Park. She was heavily pregnant and had committed suicide, mistakenly believing herself abandoned by her new lover, an army colonel.

Of all the party who had gathered at Geneva, it was Mary with whom Polidori had most sympathy. Some biographers have conjectured that John was in love with her. Charlotte Gordon in *Romantic Outlaws*, says that Polidori declared his love for Mary, only to receive the crushing response that she thought of him as a little brother. Despite being close in age, John was, in fact, slightly older. It may be that the kindly Mary had taken the fragile physician under her wing. The pair spent time together reading, specifically the Italian classics such as Tasso, and Polidori was able to use his knowledge of the language to instruct and guide Mary in the complexities of the text.

If his love was unrequited, his libido needed some outlet. In a passage, remarkably uncensored by the spinster sister, we see John waking at an unspecified hour with "pains in my loins and languor in my bones". Just a few days later, he found himself dancing waltzes and cotillons with Swiss ladies at the Odiers', doing it all over again on the following evening at Mrs Slaney's. Both nights, he stayed in town. Losing his way on the second evening, he was stopped by the police and directed home in somewhat cryptic circumstances. Andrew McConnell Stott is not the only biographer to suggest that Polidori had just left a brothel. Given

Rossi's summation of Genevan womanhood and the propriety of early relationships with multilingual expatriate ladies, John may have felt it was his only option.

The end of their stay at the Hotel d'Angleterre was now mercifully in sight. The entourage were offered the lease of a house that had belonged to Necker, the father of Madame de Staël, who will play a part in the proceedings later in the summer. As the party were making arrangements to move out of the hotel, they were afforded the unexpected chance to rent the Villa Diodati. Charles Hentsch, the banker, had done his work and had wrangled a six month lease on the house for 125 louis. Not only was it the best property they had seen since their arrival, it also had Miltonic literary connections.

Byron may have been led to believe that John Milton had stayed there whilst visiting Jean Diodati, the translator of the first Italian version of the Bible. In actuality, the villa was not constructed until 1710 but it did, most certainly, belong to the descendants of that original émigré. Byron describes it as "the most beautiful house of all around the lake located in a vineyard with the Alps behind and the Mount Jura and the lake before". Polidori echoes Byron's sentiments: "The view from his house is very fine; beautiful lake; at the bottom of the crescent is Geneva." The centre of the city is almost four kilometres (two and a half miles) from the suburb of Cologny, where the Diodati, also known as the Villa Belle Rive, can still be found in the winding Chemin de Ruth.

Despite being classified as a Swiss National Monument, the villa remains in private hands and its apartments are rented. Normally, even the gardens can only be glimpsed from beyond the boundary railings and walls. However, during 2016, in celebration of the bicentenary of that extraordinary summer, they were occasionally opened for guided tours during the evening. A small vineyard stretches impulsively downwards from the villa's classical columns which support wrought iron balconies affording views over the lake. There is a famous lithograph of Byron sat at a table on one of these balconies, pen in hand, gazing towards the Jura Mountains in an attempt to capture the muse. Although the grounds are now more meticulous with trimmed hedges outlining immaculate gravel paths and manicured lawns complete with classical pond, the position of the villa has ensured its splendid stasis. Out of the corner of one's eye, the aristocratic poet's image materializes and Mary's abandoned shoe appears under the tangled growths of a persistent vine.

The shoe was apparently lost whilst Mary was flitting between Diodati and the Maison Chapuis in the early hours of the morning. Vine growers had spotted a beaten path between the two properties and suspected an intruder. Instead, they encountered an equally surprised young woman. Years later, this story was told to Radu Florescu by a relative of the mayor of Cologny. The shoe had once been produced at a wedding in the local church as a final flourish to proceedings and proclaimed to be Mary Shelley's footwear. We agree, wholeheartedly, with Florescu's conclusion that the slipper in question must have belonged to Claire Clairmont who would have been far more likely to be returning furtively from a late night assignation with Byron.

The villa, itself, bears no commemoratory trace of the Shelleys, Claire or Polidori. The only plaque in existence attests to the poetry that Byron wrote whilst in residence. On the wall of the rectangular annex closest to the Chemin de Ruth, a stone incised with black lettering tells us, in French, the following: "English Poet, Lord Byron, author of Prisoner of Chillon, stayed in the Villa Diodati in 1816 and composed the third Canto of Childe Harold." Further along the chemin, the road opens onto a small grass-covered embankment that looks over the Diodati. In the layby at the top, an information sign welcomes visitors to Le Pré Byron or The Byron Meadow. Sparse paragraphs detail the events that led to the writing of *Frankenstein*. Alas, no mention is made of poor Polidori, but we are given an insight into Byron's turbulent state of mind when he gazed over Lake Geneva: "There was a time when I enjoyed listening to the roaring Ocean, but your gentle babbling moves me like a sister's voice blaming me for having sought evil dissipation." At the foot of the grassy hill runs the Chemin de Byron, complete with wheelie bins proudly displaying the aristocrat's name and each house number. The irony would not have been lost on Polidori.

The meadow is used on 1 August to celebrate the Swiss National Day which, fittingly, ties in with the poet's championing of Genevan patriot, François Bonivard, in the poem, *Prisoner of Chillon*. At the other end of the small parking space, firmly rooted in the middle of a flowerbed, is a boulder with the inscription "a Byron Centenaire de 1924". We were temporarily baffled by the date, eight years after the centenary of his famous stay. In fact, it should have been immediately apparent to us, but given that our focus was 1816, it was left to the archives of Geneva's *L'Impartial* newspaper to point out the obvious – the stone was commemorating Byron's death. It seems the *haute société* of 1920s Geneva attended a celebration at the Palais Eynard that included three *tableaux vivants*, recreating the interchange between the Shelleys and Byron, which even incorporated a vignette depicting Polidori's jealousy of Percy Shelley. As the newspaper article ironically recounts, the upper echelons of Genevan society were far less wary of enhancing the reputation of these scoundrel exiles than they had been over a hundred years previously.

The green-shuttered eyes of the amiable Villa Diodati would have been increasingly closed against the worsening storms that epitomized the summer of 1816. Gone were the balmy days experienced by the Shelleys at the Hotel d'Angleterre. The battened down windows and lack of light must have infuriated the prying guests at Sécheron who had rented telescopes from Monsieur Dejean in the hope of catching a glimpse of some scandalous affair amongst the Romantic circle. In the manner of Chinese whispers, white tablecloths hanging out to dry, became the dainty petticoats of Byron's harem, removed on his instruction.

The dampness of the air had turned the precipitous slopes of the villa's gardens into a treacherous mudslide. At around this time, Geneva was experiencing floods; the Rhone had burst its banks and inundated some lower-lying sections of the city. The lake level rose dramatically and dead animals contaminated the river waters. It was on 15 June that Polidori's customary clumsiness combined with the hazardous terrain to leave him incapacitated with a sprained ankle. He had jumped from a wall in a chivalrous attempt at helping Mary to climb a slope. Byron is reported to have goaded the doctor with the words "'Now you who wish to be gallant ought to jump down this small height and offer your arm'".

Polidori's youthful bravura and fondness for Mary now turned to a seething bitterness directed at his employer. Byron helped carry John indoors and even sought out a pillow with which to elevate the leg. Instead of receiving thanks for his assistance, Byron was taunted with the repost, "'I did not believe you had so much feeling'". This incident is often cited as exemplary of Polidori's petulant and childish nature. It may have been childish, but Polidori was little more than a teenager whose pride had been hurt just as much as his ankle. It is also easy to imagine the condescending manner that Byron employed in administering to the medic.

Unable to walk, Polidori took advantage of an evening at rest to have a discussion with Shelley about principles, which John describes in his diary as "whether man was to be thought merely an instrument". Traditionally, it is believed that Percy Shelley and Byron indulged in this philosophical debate on the nature of man, to which Mary was a devoted listener. However, James Rieger, in 1963 in the journal, *Studies in English Literature 1500-1900*, made some very important observations on these discussions. He is scathing of Mary's account of events published in her 1831 introduction to *Frankenstein*. She alludes to this debate about "philosophical doctrines" and he is sure that Mary confused Byron for Polidori as the participant in this conversation. Byron was competent in many fields but scientific experiment was not his forte. However, Rieger points out that Shelley was an amateur chemist and Polidori a doctor who had been witness to the cutting-edge science of the day.

Mary's introduction also mentions Erasmus Darwin who witnessed the reanimation of a worm in a glass case, as well as the experiments of the Bolognese medic, Luigi Galvani, who had been making frogs' legs twitch with an electrical current. These were not topics that Byron could have spoken on with any authority, whereas Polidori – as Rieger inidicates – had written at length on somnambulism. This theme was linked to the work of Friedrich Anton Mesmer whose theory of animal magnetism proposed a natural transference of energy between all animate and inanimate objects.

There are scholars who would possibly take issue with some of James Rieger's argument but given we, ourselves, are coaxing John's

forgotten talents into the light of day, we feel the clinching specula-
tion is that the dismissal of Polidori's play script on 15 June as "worth
nothing" prompted the doctor to then indulge in a conversation that
highlighted his expertise. Undoubtedly, these exchanges on the nature
of life would have played into the events that unfolded over the
following days.

The night sky on 16 June was electrified by the most extravagant
Alpine drama the weather could provide. The five, as John notes, all
dined and slept at the Diodati. The pieces of the potent jigsaw were
now in place for one of the most written about moments in literary
history. In reality, the events spanned a period of days, starting with
the party's reading of *Fantasmagoriana*. These were tales translated into
French from an original German collection of ghostly stories and were
subtitled *Recueil d'Histoires d'Apparitions de Spectres, Revenans, Fantômes,
etc.* To add to the heady chemistry, Mary and Shelley had, a few years'
previously, attended a theatrical enactment based on the concept of
phantasmagoriana alongside a lecture about electricity given on the
same evening.

The most plausible date for Byron's famous challenge: "We will each
write a ghost story", is during the night when these other-worldly tales
were brought to life, evidenced by the fact that John writes in his diary
on the following day, "the ghost-stories are begun by all but me". There
is no trace of any draft penned by Claire and the only spectral outline
of Shelley's attempt can be found in the poem 'Hymn to Intellectual
Beauty': "While yet a boy I sought for ghosts, and sped / Through many
a listening chamber, cave and ruin, / And starlit wood, with fearful
steps pursuing . . . "

Byron, who encouragingly said he would publish his story with
Mary's, began a vampiric tale set in the East, which is where we will
leave his story for now. Mary started to breathe life into
Frankenstein's monster. What of Polidori? He was not as quick to put
pen to paper as the others and, confusingly, Mary's aforementioned
1831 introduction to her book says that: "Poor Polidori had some ter-
rible idea about a skull-headed lady who was punished for peeping
through a key-hole . . . " If this story ever existed, it was probably in
the form of a verbal sketch. Literary history remembers *The Vampyre*

as John's contribution to the competition, which it certainly became, but it was not his only effort.

Polidori also wrote *Ernestus Berchtold; or, The Modern Oedipus* which has surprisingly few supernatural elements, instead focusing on the intriguing tale of a Swiss patriot who falls in love with a wealthy Italian's daughter, only to find a desperate familial connection. In his introduction, he clearly states:

> The tale here presented to the public is the one I began at Coligny, when Frankenstein was planned, and when a noble author having determined to descent from his lofty range, gave up a few hours to a tale of terror, and wrote the fragment published at the end of Mazeppa. Though I cannot boast of the horrible imagination of the one, or the elegant classical style of the latter, still I hope the reader will not throw mine away, because it is not equal to these.

Aside from the mocking of Byron's "lofty range" and Polidori's modesty, for the tale is very engaging, the key word here is "planned". The group's Gothic outpourings were conceived over a period of days but not completed in an instantaneous frenzy of writing. The weather and the horror continued on 18 June, which saw Lord Byron reach for a copy of Samuel Taylor Coleridge's *Christabel* and read it aloud:

> Beneath the Lamp the Lady bow'd
> And slowly roll'd her eyes around,
> Then drawing in her Breath aloud,
> Like one that shudder'd, she unbound
> The Cincture from beneath her Breast:
> Her silken Robe and inner Vest
> Dropt to her feet, and fell in View,
> Behold! her Bosom and half her Side –
> A Sight to dream of, not to tell!
> Oh shield her! shield sweet Christabel!

At this point in the evening's proceedings, an ethereal Shelley conjured a vision of a woman whose nipples had morphed into eyes. John recalls him "suddenly shrieking and putting his hands to his head". The doctor brought Shelley round from this attack of nerves, first splashing him with water then calming him with ether. The hiatus and dramatic pause had been enough to prompt Polidori into starting his own story the following day. He began *Ernestus Berchtold*, leaving *The Vampyre* for later in the summer, although Byron's fragmentary tale, from which it took inspiration, had already reached the full extent of its scant pages. The account of how the poet's vampiric Augustus Darvell, and the doctor's Lord Ruthven became confused would only come to light when *The Vampyre* appeared in print. It is true to say, however, that it was just Mary and John who pursued the challenge with any rigour.

To celebrate the bicentenary of these moments of creation, the Fondation Martin Bodmer collected a cornucopia of literary originals, artworks and associated memorabilia for its 2016 exhibition *Frankenstein: Créé des ténèbres* (Created from darkness). Our own visit coincided with this unprecedented gathering of Romantic iconography. It was with much anticipation that we walked the short distance from the Diodati to the street bearing the Swiss bibliophile collector's name. His Fondation is located in a seemingly modest yet solid structure whose straight roofline is broken by the heavy-lidded corner projections that add a touch of grandeur.

Deceptively, the modern day exhibition space greatly extends the building's footprint, being tucked in the cool recesses of an enlarged basement area. The modernist entrance displayed the exhibition's credentials with the black stencilled lettering of Mary Shelley's creation broken and scattered across a cerise background. We were immediately jolted from the contemporary to the nineteenth century when confronted by four artworks we had come to know well from their reproductions in many biographies. From right to left, Percy Bysshe Shelley, Mary Shelley, Lord Byron and John William Polidori were lining up to welcome the visitor to the time of their young lives.

From an ornately gilded frame, Polidori is portrayed looking away from the viewer, his eyes focusing on distant thoughts. A white cravat allows his bohemian high collar to drape over the edge of his black cloak. A curl from John's profuse, dark and gently rippling hair falls over his forehead, almost touching the pronounced eyebrows, accentuated by a pale complexion. The hint of a five o'clock shadow plays around impassive lips and an oval chin. His neck, elongated by the cravat, gives John a confident presence, every inch the dandy poet he wanted to be. Yet there is a limpid sadness in his brown eyes, an acknowledgement of life's treacherous course. Change only the clothing and Polidori could easily be the shoe-gazing lead singer of an indie band.

John's portrait was painted by F.G. Gainsford and normally resides in the British National Portrait Gallery, as does the Richard Westall image of Byron that was also on loan to the Bodmer. Milord wears a red jacket and Georgian shirt held together with a broach. Seemingly unperturbed, chin resting on his hand, the profile is overly posed. As we know from Thorvaldsen's bust, George Gordon could be a difficult sitter who would insist on an attitude designed to invoke the muse. It is Byron's dark hair, pale skin and curls that have evoked a comparison with the younger Polidori. However, the poet's features are more fragile and his voluptuous mouth seems to be capable of curling with deep passion or contempt.

The portraits of the Shelleys are altogether more otherworldly. Mary's portrait, having been painted after the tragic events of her life had unfolded, conveys melancholy despite a small smile on her lips. Her eyes engage with the viewer in a knowing way, implying a worldly intelligence and a female strength of resolve. Percy's image, created by Amelia Curran in 1819, is sprite-like, delicate and overly didactic. With quill in hand, Shelley almost seems to bleed his poetry, giving every ounce of energy to his words.

Naturally, the first scripts we encountered, housed in glass cabinets, were the original drafts of *Frankenstein*. The faded writing, with its many annotations, crossed the pages in all directions with the energy of a writer intent on doing justice to her craft. The years condensed to allow us the sudden apparition of Mary at a window in the Maison Chapuis, discussing the application of science and the humanity of man. Letters followed the manuscripts, thoughts that had passed between Byron, the Shelleys and their wider literary circle. The hand written word gave way to first and inscribed editions of their many works; the most poignant inscription, added to the inner leaf of Mary's edition gifted to the poet, was this short dedication belying a deeper meaning: "To Byron from the author".

The last wall of the exhibition contained a pixilated black and white image depicting the accoutrements of vampiric lore. Centre stage lay a copy of *The Vampyre*, opened at the title sheet. It was adorned with the simple subtitle – *A Tale*, in addition to the publisher's details and the emphatic admission that it was printed in London. No name was attached to the work; the binding remained obscured from view. It was left to the surrounding panels to tell the story of its unusual birth. After 200 years, Polidori was taking his rightful place amongst the party of refugee *littérateurs* gathered in Geneva.

Hours had passed in the Bodmer basement. Emerging from the shady cool into the brilliant sunshine of a Cologny summer required a beer and a chance to digest all we had seen. Sitting in a small café opposite the church, we realized our journey, timed to coincide with the bicentenary, had brought us closer to the opaque nights of June 1816 than we could have imagined. The ink, faded to a bloodied copper brown on the pages still held something of each writer's personality. Despite the ease of access to digitized manuscripts online, no computerized reproduction could ever quite match seeing them first-hand, without the distancing filter of technology.

Helpful to the reader of Polidori's diary is the sketch the doctor made of his rooms at the Diodati, showing his bed chamber next to a space he labels the picture-gallery. As interior access is no longer permitted, the sketch combined with old photographs is the only recourse we have to imagine the days John spent resting his ankle inside the house. Radu Florescu includes a 1975 photograph of the main living room in his book. Pictures are much in evidence and framed in heavy gilt, as is a large mirror that dominates one wall, reflecting light from the lake and the Louis XV-style furnishings. The elaborate cornicing, crystal droplets of the chandelier and tied drapes at the veranda windows give an aristocratic note to what could have been an unassuming room.

Frustratingly, just as Polidori picks up pace with his novel writing, his diary tails off into clipped inconsistencies as can be seen from this supposed explanation he was given of a Swiss religious battle: "Chief advances; calls the other. Calls himself and other fools, for battles will not persuade of his being wrong. Other agreed . . . " Adding to John's sense of listless lack of purpose was the news that Byron and Shelley had proposed a boating trip around the lake in search of the locations mentioned in Rousseau's novel *Julie, ou la nouvelle Héloïse*. Byron, who knew passages of the text by heart, had prompted an enthused Percy to also immerse himself in the Swiss author's philosophical writing.

Rousseau started to write *Julie* whilst staying with Madame d'Epinay near Paris before returning to Geneva. It tells the story of Julie d'Etange who falls in love with her tutor, St Preux. The disapproving father insists she marry a befittingly moneyed suitor instead, prompting the lovelorn tutor to disappear. When St Preux eventually returns, the inevitable rekindling of their passion results in a clash between convention and authentic feeling. The story unfolds around the lake with Vevey and the wood at Clarens being key destinations. Rousseau described the thought processes behind the novel in his autobiographical *Confessions*:

> Amidst so many prejudices and factitious passions, one must know how to analyze properly the human heart, in order to disentangle the true feelings of nature. A delicacy of tact is necessary, which can only be acquired by intercourse with the great world, in order to feel, if I may so venture to say, the delicacies of heart of which this work is full.

The novel, with its challenging of societal norms and the proposition that one should follow one's heart even if that path diverges from accepted moral values, attracted the attention of Catholic censors and was placed on the Vatican's List of Prohibited Books (the Index Librorum Prohibitorum). Calvinist Geneva was equally shocked, but for our Romantic apostates the text was a call to arms.

The prospect of a literary excursion full of intellectual conversation would have thrilled Polidori as much as the poets, but he was not to be invited. The pretext, of course, was his damaged ankle, but we suspect this was merely a ruse to leave him behind as the pair could have easily postponed the trip until John was able to walk sufficiently well. It goes without saying that Mary and Claire would not have been considered part of this male-bonding process. A curious anecdote, with its only source being Thomas Moore, purports to show Polidori's state of mind at being excluded.

If we are to believe Moore in his entirety, John's temper, always close to the surface, burst forth in vitriol at not being included in the poets' excursion. Byron, ever conscious of his superior status, was indignant at being challenged on a decision that was of no concern to an employee. Moore has Polidori limping to his room, certain that his conduct must lead to a dismissal. Apparently, the doctor was so distraught, he drew poison from his medicine cabinet and was on the point of writing a suicide note when Byron entered his room and stumbled upon the scene. Soothing words from the aristocrat dissuaded John from taking any rash action. With no corroboratory evidence, we will never know if this incident happened as stated, or indeed, if Polidori's intention was merely attention-seeking.

Byron and Shelley left on 22 June, stopping at the relevant settlements on the shores of Léman. The apogee of their trip was the bosquet de Julie at Clarens. Whilst discussing the nature of religion, love and man, Byron halted the conversation with the words: "'Thank God, Polidori is not here!'" John would have been the eager puppy intent on gaining the attention and approval of his master. The comment is evidence of the depth to which their relationship had sunk. Polidori may have had valuable contributions to make, but Byron did not want to hear them from the mouth of a man whose personality clearly clashed with his own.

Ironically, if John had not been so desperate to be part of the club, he would have realized that time away from the poets and in the less competitive atmosphere created by Mary and Claire, was beneficial to his health, wellbeing and art. His diary mentions regular dinners with the ladies and time to talk in a relaxed manner – "Dined down with Mrs S and Miss CC", "after at Mrs S", "went to Mrs S; Miss C talked of a soliloquy", "All day at Mrs S". It is also during these days that Polidori makes his first mention of a Countess Breuss, whilst dining with Rossi. The Countess will come to play a part in the unfolding story as the summer progresses.

On the rain-drenched 2 July, a day after Byron and Shelley had returned from their trip, fresh from a boating disaster which saw Percy nearly lose his life, John's diary comes to an abrupt halt with the words "In the evening to Mrs S". The entries would only resume at the beginning of September with these reasons for his silence: "Not written my Journal till now through neglect and dissipation." What happened during the intervening weeks?

Polidori had begun to throw himself into the Genevan social scene with even more vigour. The most notable soirees he frequented, also attended by Byron, were held by Madame de Staël at her mansion in Coppet, on the opposite side of the lake from Cologny and a handful of kilometres from the French border. De Staël was a celebrated writer who had already published a considerable collection of journals, biographies, essays and novels. She periodically retired to Coppet as a retreat from the world of political machinations and lived there with the considerably younger Albert de Rocca whom she married in secret. Frequent guests were the writer, Charles Victor de Bonstetten, and the translator of Shakespeare, August Wilhelm von Schlegel. While Byron took to some guests, he had a virulent dislike of others, calling Schlegel "the Dousterswivel of Madame de Staël", an epithet that took some deciphering until we discovered that it meant a two-faced schemer.

John, who attended three of these evening gatherings at Coppet, wryly noticed the relationship between de Staël and Byron – at some turns playful, at others full of candour but always with an intellectual rigour. Polidori was aware of her tendency to advise Byron and to speak freely in a manner that he knew he would never be able to achieve. For the lady of the house, Coppet must have seemed a world away from Paris and the tortuous events of the French Revolution. Her chateau remains largely unchanged, although our view was restricted by the lateness of the hour and the padlocked iron railings that barred entry.

We were able to see the landscaped grounds and mature trees partially obscuring the pink façade and green-shuttered windows of a building far grander in dimension and design than the Villa Diodati. Like Byron's residence, the property is privately owned but unlike the Diodati, it is possible to take a guided tour within the confines of a strict timetable. Sadly, through poor planning, we missed the opportunity to view Madame de Stael's furniture, paintings, textiles and possessions, lovingly kept by the Fondation Othenin d'Haussonville.

Simply reading about the interior of the chateau conveys the weight of literary and cultural heritage carried by the owners. It was a weight that Polidori keenly felt, especially as his age and boyish good looks belied his learning. To prove his provenance as a doctor, he even went to the length of presenting de Stael with a copy of his Edinburgh dissertation. In such company, John was never able to relax. This was not the case, however, at the parties hosted by Countess Breuss at Genthod, once again a short row across from Cologny.

The Maison d'Abraham Gallatin was home to a plethora of poetic enticements including such affectations as a moated island and Moorish follies. It became the venue for much laughter, dancing and flirting amongst a selection of guests who varied in both outlook and age. The garden's bowers provided the backdrop to plays and monologues delivered in the costumes that much pleased the countess. There is some dispute about her origins, and we have seen her name in numerous forms, including the anglicized Bruce and the more Russian, Bryus. Andrew McConnell Stott, in his essay on the events of the summer, plumps for the most likely story – that she was the daughter of a Russian courtier who was the wife of the governor general of Moscow.

At least twice a week, John would make his way across the lake to see the woman who, it was claimed, maintained two husbands that were conveniently separated by much distance – one living in Russia and one in Venice. The guests were an eclectic bunch: a hypochondriac lady fond of medicaments, an abbot, Charles Saladin – formerly of Napoleon's army, Foncet – a Piedmontese officer, and a mixture of *comtesses*, ladies of note and aspiring *mademoiselles*. In a diary entry, harking back to those balmy summer nights, John lists the names of the players in one of the amateur theatricals that took place. Amongst them is a certain Madame Brelaz.

The lady in question was Portuguese and accompanied by her daughter who clearly frowned on the attentions that Polidori was paying the older woman. He even confides in a later journal entry that he was "in love with her; I think fond of me too", but in the next breath, he also gives us the throw-away line "Clemann – got half in love with her; nice daughter". The atmosphere of the soirees must have been laden with an undertow of sensuality, if not simple sexual attraction.

The sharing of initials and the same dance floor partners between the ladies Breuss and Brelaz has led to some confusion in accounts that have dealt with Polidori's summer frivolities. Many Byron biographies make casual references to the lady who encouraged John to expand the theme that Byron had briefly introduced in his story fragment. We have seen both Breuss and Brelaz take the role as the reanimator of *The Vampyre*. Our personal preference is for the "dark lady", the Portuguese beauty of his imagination and his reality. He may have flirted with Countess Breuss but does not commit his feelings to paper. He cannot have been so circumspect when talking of Madame Brelaz, as Claire infers that sending Polidori "to the lady he loves" would have been a good way to remove his presence from the Diodati, thereby allowing her to sneak away more easily after an assignation with Byron.

Even though John was dedicating time to pleasure and literature, as befitting his age, the spat with Byron had prompted him to take his duties more seriously. However, in doing so, his laissez faire attitude to minutiae caused the rest of the staff some trouble. The Swiss servant, Berger, complained of his reckless use of the horses, leaving one lame; he was also too free with the household money in renting carriages. On one occasion, whilst driving a gig with his partner in crime – a Welshman called Lloyd whom he had met at one of Countess Breuss' parties – the pair crashed into a horse and cart leading to an altercation with the cart's owner that was only broken up by a passing carriage.

The fuse of Polidori's short temper was once again lit by the artfulness of a local chemist. Byron, with his extreme dieting habits and alcohol consumption, was often in need of a remedy to settle his heartburn. The early-nineteenth century drug of choice for such a complaint was magnesia and the poet had been coping without since our doctor had broken the last bottle in Karlsruhe. Dutifully, Polidori went to Geneva in search of a new supply and found himself ripped off by the pharmacist. A retrospective diary entry tells the tale: "Found it bad by experiment of sulphuric acid colouring it red-rose colour."

Castan, the apothecary, was called from his establishment to witness the proof of the bad quality of his product, but refused to exit the premises. John, always sensitive to a slight or humiliation, was quick to forcibly remove the reluctant man so he could watch the discoloration of the magnesia; however, in so doing, Polidori managed to break the chemist's spectacles. The sulking shop owner firstly remained rooted to the spot and steadfastly ignored the result of the experiment. He then recruited two friendly physicians and they importuned a no doubt despairing Byron, telling him of Polidori's conduct.

John was hauled before a local court to account for his behaviour. His diary gives the details and demonstrates one of the least endearing qualities of his character:

> Brought me to trial before five judges; had an advocate to plead. I pleaded for myself; laughed at the advocate. Lost his cause on the plea of calumny; made me pay 12 florins for the broken spectacles and costs. Magnesia chiefly alumina, as proved by succenate and carbonate of ammonia.

Although Polidori was right in his assumption of having been duped, he was arrogant enough to represent himself in a foreign court and to actively laugh at the qualified advocate pleading for the prosecution. John says that his allegedly slanderous behaviour was dismissed by the court, yet we suspect, if he had been more humble in his approach, he would not have had to pay the twelve florins and costs for a case that he had supposedly won.

This incident can only have added to the tensions escalating amongst the circle of friends. During one of their boating excursions, Polidori had even threatened – as he blithely puts it in his journal – "to shoot S one day on the water". The "S" is, of course, Percy Shelley and Thomas Moore informs us that the episode was prompted by the outcome of a sailing race. This outburst was a release for pent up jealousy caused by continuous exclusion and cruel humour. John was used to the nickname "Polly", affectionately applied by his sisters, but Byron's extension to "Polly Dolly" was designed for mockery. In response to John's offer of a duel, Shelley declined, but Moore is certain that Byron scornfully suggested that he would take his place.

Well into August, the Shelleys, Claire, Byron and Polidori continued to spend time together at the Diodati. This would come to an abrupt end for Mary on 13 August when, after the usual visit, her diary records one simple but stark word – "war". There is no evidence as to the cause for such a dramatic response, but it is clear that tempers on all sides were becoming frayed. Even Percy was rather disillusioned with some of Byron's more unseemly traits. Into this atmosphere stepped Matthew Gregory Lewis, more commonly known as Monk Lewis, owing to the popularity of his Gothic novel, *The Monk*.

Lewis added to the macabre mix by reading some of his own translations of Goethe's *Faust*, and no doubt regaling the Romantics with the origins of his sinister friar. The hugely popular book had brought Matthew a certain notoriety given the subject matter of the text. Ambrosio, the central character, struggles with his monastic vows in a Capuchin friary near Madrid. Ambition leads to obsession, rape and murder until he is forced into a Faustian pact with the devil that could never end well.

Finally, on 26 August, Hobhouse and Scrope Davies arrived in Geneva pushing Polidori's star ever further from the halo of the moon. Three days later, mirroring their departure from London's Piccadilly, Byron, his two friends and the doctor rode out of Cologny in the direction of Chamonix. This trip was to be the end of the road for Byron and Polidori. As before, Davies sat with the poet in his carriage, whilst John was left to make conversation with Hobhouse whose opinion of Polidori had only worsened. There is scant reference to the journey in John's retrospective diary entry for 5 September, a simple "we went to Chamounix" followed by an enumeration of the places visited; perhaps the reflection of a less than happy time.

Hobhouse has a far more fulsome account of the trip, describing the party's exit from the vale of Chamonix "by the ridge of the noble ravine of the Arve on our right, taking many a look back at the majestic snows of Mont Blanc and her craggy needles rushing into the clouds". They reached the mountain via the French border at Annemasse, then by way of Bonneville and Sallenches. We approached western Europe's highest peak from the Italian border and the Monte Bianco tunnel, costing an intake of breath inducing forty-four euros twenty. As we had decided to view Mont Blanc on the way back from tracking Polidori's footsteps in Italy, we had unwittingly timed our arrival perfectly. As we sailed through the arrow-straight tunnel, half of France was queueing to access their own slice of *la dolce vita*.

The Italian approach to the mountain is up-close and personal, whereas exiting the tunnel on the French side, once the hairpin bends have been negotiated, you are presented with an extensive panorama that runs parallel to the road and offers perfect views of Hobhouse's "craggy needles". There were no clouds to obscure our view of the peaks, stark against the background of an azure Italian sky. John was not so fortunate with his travel arrangements and noted that things were "so bad we left". It is not clear whether he was talking about the weather, the route they had chosen to walk, or the atmosphere amongst the participants.

Hobhouse's diary contains several entries that refer to John's conversation. It seems that the doctor wanted to impress Byron's friend with his knowledge of geology, pointing out rock stratification and the difference between the theories of Hutton and Werner who had disputed publically about the igneous nature of rocks. John declared both theories valid. The doctor felt on firmer ground when he told Hobhouse of his opinions regarding the goitres that were so common in the Alpine regions. According to Polidori, they were caused by bad air, not bad water which, unfortunately, is a complete fallacy as we now know that they were due to a lack of iodine in the water.

Hobhouse tolerated Polidori's boyish enthusiasm but was doubtless saving up points of irritation that he could relay to Byron in an attempt to rid them of his presence once and for all. Byron would not need much persuading as he had already decided that he had no need of a medic, let alone one who had threatened a duel, appeared before the courts, taken liberties with the household expenses, quarrelled with his friends and, possibly, even threatened suicide. In an inverse reflection of these deficits, we see a young, highly-strung Polidori dealing with aristocratic hauteur, biting sarcasm, mockery and a lack of appreciation for his considerable brain.

Having returned to Cologny from their Chamonix excursion, Hobhouse felt rather ill. Busying himself with letters home and the parcelling of plants for his mother, he complained of uneasiness in the throat and head. Polidori was called and, as reported in Hobhouse's diary, diagnosed that he was going to die of either apoplexy or pneumonia. It is not clear whether the doctor actually meant this or was enacting a delicious revenge on his nemesis.

By 15 September, matters had reached a head and John mournfully writes:

> LB determined upon our parting, – not upon any quarrel, but on account of our not suiting. Gave me £70; 50 for 3 months and 20 for voyage. Paid away a great deal, and then thought of setting off: determined for Italy. Madame de Staël gave me three letters. Madame B wept, and most seemed sorry.

Hobhouse was the go-between who aided the doctor to settle his accounts with Byron and pronounced that Polidori did not meet Madame de Staël's definition of a happy man. His retelling of John's departure finishes with this acid drop of scorn we mentioned in Chapter 1: "He is anything but an amiable man, and has a most unmeasured ambition, as well as inordinate vanity. The true ingredients of misery . . . " Leaving aside the "unmeasured ambition", this could almost be a description of Byron and it is as well to remember that Hobhouse, at thirty years of age, was secure in his life and status; John was twenty-one, unemployed and lost.

CHAPTER FIVE

Italy
The Austrian Soldier's Hat

John's last evening was spent with his Genthod friends, watching them perform *C'est le même*. Although he had told them of his intention to leave at the beginning of the party, only "Madame B", presumably Madame Brelaz, appears to have received an intimate farewell. As the night drew to a close, a solitary Polidori stole away from the revelries, too upset to make his goodbyes.

The following morning saw him leave Cologny and his employ as Byron's doctor. He wasted no time in setting off as the dawn broke and headed for St Gingolph, passing into Savoy, then part of the Kingdom of Sardinia. John was on foot and carried with him few possessions. As he walked past Meillerie, he pulled a letter from his pocket and read the parting words of Madame Brelaz. Along with her tender goodbye she had included some verses but it was the prose that caused his tears to fall.

After sleeping in Gingolph, he re-entered Switzerland and "crossed to Chillon". By using the word "crossed", we assume he must have taken a boat the short distance from Port-Valais to Montreux, rather than walk the serrated path around the tip of Lac Léman. The Château de Chillon, which was Polidori's destination, lies some two kilometres outside Montreux and is the true tourist honeypot for the lakeside region. John would have already been aware of its fame thanks to Byron's visit with Shelley and the time his employer had spent constructing verses on the theme of the prisoner, Bonivard.

The approach to the castle from the water is a marketing executive's dream. Clichéd it may be, but it is impossible for a creative soul not to

The Stockalper Palace, Brig, S. Edwards

The Semplon Pass, R. Gerber, Pixabay

Statue of Galvani, Piazza
Luigi Galvani, Bologna,
S. Edwards

The Lungarno, Pisa,
A. Edwards

be moved by the vision. Representations in art are legion and our imagination had been pre-empted by the painting of the scene created by Gustave Courbet which we had viewed at the Wallraf-Richartz Museum in Cologne. Courbet, better known for his graphic portrayal of female genitalia, *L'Origine du monde*, hanging in the Musée d'Orsay, completed his Chillon in 1873. Little has changed since the Frenchman in exile put brush to canvas.

Although we approached from the Vevey road, the castle still seems to be moored on the lake, its medieval towers both solidly rooted yet ephemeral against the permanence of the Alps. The oldest references to the structure date back to the beginning of the eleventh century, but most of the expansion took place under the rule of Peter II of Savoy in the thirteenth. The road from Montreux hugs the lake and is jammed against a cliff-face, making parking somewhat of a headache. The medieval ambience is rather broken by the necklace of vehicles but once you have left the tarmac and set foot on the cobbled approach, modernity falls away.

The lake forms a natural moat and access to the castle is via a wooden bridge that leads to an inner courtyard. We climbed each tower, looking through the narrow openings that gave perfectly framed views of the lake, the mountains or the opposing turrets capped with their picturesque conical hats. Covered walkways connect the towers and float above the courtyards below. The stone enclosures are softened with the addition of abundant floral display and are usually populated with camera-toting visitors. Such agreeable scenes hide a brutal past, which was difficult to conjure on a cloudless July day.

The cobbles would have run with the blood of women tortured and eventually burnt as witches. Even one of the beams, now attractively patina'd with age, would have been set aside for the hangman's noose with its suspended rotting corpse. The only part of the castle that still holds a hint of this sadistic atmosphere is the dungeon, located below the lapping waters. On entering the compartments leading to the prison, we were greeted with the more reassuring sight of stacked wine barrels, the contents of which can be purchased from the obligatory gift shop.

Further into the complex of rooms, the atmosphere dampens as the final chamber, propped by stone pillars, widens into the bowels of the castle. On one of the pillars is a carved signature, singled out from the others by the addition of a protective glass and iron frame. Clearly visible in capitals are the deeply carved letters spelling the name "Byron". It is open to debate as to whether this was made by the actual hand of the poet or some unscrupulous agent of the Swiss proto-tourist industry trying to cash in on the fame of the poem, *The Prisoner of Chillon*.

In addition to Byron's letters and verses plus Polidori's diary, we were also carrying with us an 1887 copy of Baedeker's Switzerland – the latter being valued more for its atmosphere than the information it contained. Needless to say, the guide refers to Byron's poetry evoking Bonivard's gaol, which we quote here: "There are seven pillars of Gothic mould, / In Chillon's dungeons deep and old, / There are seven columns, massy and grey, / Dim with a dull imprisoned ray, / A sunbeam which hath lost its way . . . " The Baedeker, however, makes the mistake of quoting from the 'Sonnet on Chillon', implying the lines are from 'The Prisoner' – a frequent error. The opening of the sonnet is a timeless tribute to those persecuted for their opinions and a recognition of the human ability to overcome hardship: "Eternal Spirit of the chainless mind! / Brightest in dungeons, Liberty! Thou art . . . "

Despite this slight faux pas, our 1887 guide is quick to point out the following:

> It is an error to identify Bonivard, the victim to the tyranny of the Duke of Savoy, and confined by him in these gloomy dungeons for six years, with Byron's 'Prisoner of Chillon'. The author calls his poem a fable, and when he composed it he was not aware of the history of Bonivard, or he would, as he himself states, have attempted to dignify the subject by an endeavour to celebrate his courage and virtue.

Interestingly, the sonnet is the more informed of the two pieces as it was written after Byron had received a detailed history of Bonivard from Madame de Staël's husband. It is easy to see how confusion arose as the sonnet, composed later on, was placed before the poem in printed editions.

It is clear from an entry in Polidori's diary that he knew Chillon had held Bonivard for six years in the 1530s and he was able to see various items used to torture the prisoners, including a pulley that would wrench arms from sockets. François Bonivard is viewed today as a Genevan patriot, political activist and a champion of the Protestant Reformation, although his reputation has been somewhat tarnished by the inference that he was a libertine, despite his priestly vocation. Rumours of wild parties abound and his fourth and last wife, Catherine, was an unfrocked nun who was arrested for immorality and infidelity after she had married François. He tried to have her absolved but without success. In evangelically Swiss fashion, the former bride of Christ and the lover she had taken were executed; Catherine was drowned in the River Rhone and he was beheaded.

Polidori was inspired, just as his recent employer had been, by this visit to Chillon, choosing it as a setting in *Ernestus Berchtold*. He may have begun this story whilst in Geneva, but it was still clearly a work in progress, as many of the locations in the tale were as yet unknown to John. The eponymous Ernestus is befriended by Olivieri, the pair being former comrades in arms, and is subsequently corrupted by his friend's debased lifestyle. At a certain point in the story, Berchtold is arrested as an outlaw, having fought against the occupying French. He is taken to the Château de Chillon and thrown into one of the dungeon's cells:

> Into this narrow space I was forced to enter. It was not sufficiently long for me to lie down at full length, and the barred grating, which, far above my reach, was intended in mockery to represent a window, received no reflected light from the dark floor of Bonniva's prison. I heard the doors fasten one after another.
>
> Beneath the slowly sounding wave I was cut off from humanity; the monotonous dashing against the castle's base alone broke the dread silence; it seemed like the loud note of the moments in nature's last hour. My spirits fled, and I leant against the stones to which I was chained, with hands clasped, and my eyes painfully straining, as if they sought at last to see the real horrors of my dwelling.

Ernestus escapes using his own ingenuity and a file, slipped into his hand by a child during a rare moment above ground. Berchtold's adventures in central southern Switzerland and Italy are a mirror of Polidori's own wanderings. From Chillon, John walked through the region now known as the Parc naturel regional Gruyère Pays-d'Enhaut, passing through Rougemont until he reached Weissenbach and Boltigen. At the edge of the Parc, the Canton of Vaud gives way to the Canton of Bern, marking the linguistic border that John observes in this dejected comment: "and they begin their German; found it difficult to go on". From the easily understood French of Geneva, he was plunged back into struggling with the Teutonic tongue he had been happy to leave behind at the Rhine.

By 19 September, he had reached Thun, whose panorama he had witnessed months previously in Basle. The following day, still dogged by a low mood, he found the time to write to Madame Brelaz, his uncle in Italy and his father, amongst others. The letter to Gaetano reveals much that was hidden or removed from his diary and is worth quoting at length:

> Your letter gave me pleasure; and I was indeed in want of some just then, for I was in agitation for my parting from Lord Byron. We have parted, finding that our tempers did not agree. He proposed it, and it was settled. There was no immediate cause, but a continued series of slight quarrels. I believe the fault, if any, has been on my part; I am not accustomed to have a master, and therefore my conduct was not free and easy. I found on settling accounts that I had 70 napoleons; I therefore determined to walk over Italy, and (seeing the medical establishments) see if there proves a good opportunity to settle myself, so that I hope I am still off your hands for nine months . . .

His father must have been waiting to receive such a letter, convinced as he was that Byron would be a most unsuitable employer for his son. Gaetano had had the sense to leave Alfieri before he was pushed, whereas John had allowed his situation to spiral downwards until, fed by the mutterings of Hobhouse, Shelley and Claire Clairmont, Byron felt he had no choice but to dismiss him. Polidori's letter brings a self-effacing clarity to his dismissal, as he takes pains to point out the role of his own defects, although we cannot help but feel that part of his rationale in doing so was to deny his father's opinion that Byron would be the nightmare master he proved to be.

We also learn from the letter that it was John's intention to head for Italy, but he would have to negotiate the Bernese Oberland on foot before reaching his destination. John's appreciation of Thun, with its covered arcades, was marred by the fact that the stray dog he had adopted for company had eaten something poisonous and was violently sick, prompting more tears that always seemed to be so close to the surface during his walk. To reach Interlaken, Polidori skirted the northern banks of the Thunersee and found an inn at Unterseen which is separated from Interlaken by the Aare River. The guesthouse had two English visitors, thus enabling conversation but it did little to dispel his loneliness.

Despite his melancholy, or perhaps because of it, John was able to write copious notes in his diary, appreciating the panorama before him: "I went to the bridge at Interlachen to see the view coming between two beautiful isolated crags." We drove along the Höheweg through the centre of town; the road being flanked by a park that announced the irresistible presence of John's isolated peaks. Their sheer magnetism made focussing on the road ahead somewhat difficult. We headed in a southerly direction towards of the end of the Höheweg, looking for the most plausible location of the bridge that crossed the Aare. The doctor was lodging in Unterseen and two bridges cross the river at this point, the nearer of the two conveying the Bahnhofstrasse to its destination. The structure has evidently been modernized but the view is the closest match for Polidori's description.

On the bridge, he met an army marshal who, after completing his training, had wandered Mitteleuropa in search of experience, in much the same way as John was now doing, although our Anglo-Italian was heading south. To save his already battered feet, he decided to cadge a ride with the two Englishmen from the inn on their excursion to Grindelwald, initially heading for the Lauterbrunnen Valley, specifically to see the Staubbach Waterfall which he describes accurately as "a bare cataract of 900 feet high, becoming vapour before it arrives". Returning via Grindelwald, Polidori finds himself in high country, name-dropping some of Europe's most famous mountains: the Jungfrau, the Eiger, and the Wetterhorn.

It seems that Byron and Hobhouse had been of the same mind. As John's *"char-à-banc"* hurtled back towards the twin lakes of Thun and Brienz, the poet and his friend were heading for Grindelwald. Polidori simply says that "we saluted". He must have felt a pang of jealousy and loss. A cursory glance through Byron's writings and Hobhouse's journal shows that this trip from Geneva was a highlight for the two friends and their obvious merriment would have cut to the core. Byron confided to the page these words of contentment: "In the weather for this tour (of 13 days), I have been very fortunate – fortunate in a companion (Mr H^e) – fortunate in our prospects, and exempt from even the little petty accidents and delays . . . " He had never said anything approaching these words in relation to Polidori.

Back in Interlaken, the doctor found his money was swiftly running out. He feigned disinterest in the continued companionship of his two English compatriots, although this was probably due to his inability to match their spending. Once again, he set off on his own, passing through Meiringen and heading south to Guttannen and beyond "through the wildest and most sublime scenery". John finds his descriptive voice at this lowest of ebbs:

> The river's bed the most magnificent imaginable, cut deep and narrow into the solid rock, sinuous, and continually accompanied by cascades, and amazing bold and high single-arched bridges. Snow covering in some parts the whole bed of the river, and so thick and strong that even huge stones have fallen without injuring its crust.

The road from Guttannen leads over the Grimsel Pass which, as its name suggests, has a gloomy and ominous quality. The surrounding landscape is stripped of all but the most essential vegetation – bare rock and descending mists add to the sense of *finis mundi*. It was in these detached environs that John wrote the lines that he would append to his collection of poetry, *Ximenes, The Wreath and Other Poems*, released in 1819. Latter day critics have acknowledged his accomplished prose style, evident in *The Vampyre* and *Ernestus Berchtold*, yet Polidori, unadvisedly, persisted with his poetic aspirations. Nevertheless, 'Written at the Grimsel' conveys his state of mind:

In vain I seek these solitary rocks,
Which seemed to leave no trace upon their side
For man to tread upon. – These enduring blocks
Of the world's masonry, o'er which storms glide
Powerless, unmoved stern in their might yet stand,
And leave no room for man's destructive hand. –
Yet I am vainly hid within their breast,
They cannot breathe on me their quiet rest –
Man's passions will intrude, man's wants assail . . .

The poem continues by evoking young love, the muse and this telling line on the desire for recognition: "Oh why still in my soul, those hopes of fame, / Which brought the sigh when busy morning came . . . "

Literary fame had never been further from his reach. With these wistful thoughts, Polidori descended in the only direction possible, following the line of the valley to "Viesch". John was not always accurate in his German spelling of place names and in this instance he replaced the initial 'F' with a 'V'. Consequently, we drove the Furkastrasse next to the Rhone, looking for a location beginning with a 'V', bypassing the obvious name of Feisch. In the manner of comedian Frankie Howerd, we had already raised a childish Anglo Saxon titter at Wankdorf but by the time we had seen signs to the Furka Pass and Bitsch we were helpless with laughter.

Feisch has none of the grimness of the Grimsel; the Hotel du Glacier dominates the centre of the village and wooden chalets, complete with bright geraniums, overlook the milky waters of the river, with more flower boxes clinging to the safety railings. It is quintessential in its Swissness. The few shops displayed expensive out of season ski gear and walking boots for the serious hiker. Polidori was still suffering with his inadequate footwear for such rocky terrain, although the crags had lessened by the time he had reached Feisch. The descent to Brig is typical Alpine meadow.

At this point, John fell in with two students from the Jesuit's College. Despite having little money, he gave some to one of the penniless would-be priests. He was happier in the company of a curate he met in Brig itself. Owing to his days spent at Ampleforth College, he was able to converse in Latin, a language finally fading as the lingua franca of educated Europe. It must have been a curiosity for any passing Swiss German to hear a twenty-one year old Anglo-Italian speaking in such an archaic tongue to a man three times his age about the recent French invasion and Swiss reprisal.

Brig is dominated by the seventeenth-century Stockalper Palace, instantly recognizable by its three towers topped with copper spheres in the manner of pearl onions speared on cocktail sticks. The town proudly boasts that the palace is Switzerland's largest private Baroque building, although it does house a museum. In the courtyard, we spotted a bright yellow and black horse-drawn coach, now consigned to the shelter of a corner arch, but which would have once delivered the post and people over the Simplon Pass. Kaspar von Stockalper, the creator of the building, made his money from Simplon trade making it a fitting resting place for the carriage.

Polidori makes no mention of the palace, even in conversation with the curate, being far more concerned with his forthcoming trek over the mountains and knowing full-well that he would not be able to afford to take advantage of a carriage ride. He sought advice from the priest who knew the Simplon well, with the outcome that the elderly man accompanied him to the edge of town, keen to put him on the right track. John had made a favourable impression, as he so often did when not feeling pressured to put on an act: "Left me in sight of Brieg, telling me he hoped to see me again in heaven."

The modern road over the Simplon is still daunting, with its multiple curves and impatient traffic waiting to overtake the lorries delivering luxury goods to Italy. Stretches of the road are completely deserted and others condensed with vehicles. To attempt such a journey on foot left us full of admiration, even if John did have the benefit of Napoleon's new road. He climbed to a hospice where he was able to take a monastic cell from one of the monks and obtain some much needed bread, cold meat and wine. We passed through defunct customs posts amidst pockets of snow in the north-facing crevices, overhanging the "granite galleries" that so impressed Polidori.

The Italian–Swiss border now dissects the road between Zwischbergen and Iselle. Signs proclaiming Italia encircled by yellow European stars welcome the traveller; Polidori had no such indication that he was treading the soil of his ancestors. Tired, aching and bewildered, he approached a young villager and, in his best German, asked for directions. The response "'Non capisco'" was more than he could have hoped for and he tells his diary that he wanted to hug the young man. With "ruined" feet, he found a filthy lodging and fell into a deep sleep.

The first town of any size he reached was Domodossola. Today, it is the railway hub that connects Italy with Brig. A passenger stepping onto the train at the immaculate Swiss station and disembarking at Domodossola could not help but notice the difference – the Italian town is rougher round the edges, less compact and content to haphazardly sprawl into its Alpine meadows. For all this, it makes a more relaxed and less demanding impression on the visitor. We found a hotel on the outskirts overlooking houses that were a villa-chalet hybrid. Our walk into the centre was along tree-lined streets towards the cobbled heart, sadly suffering from a patchwork of neglect, hurriedly filled with tarmac and dangerous to both car tyre and high-heel.

John checked-in to a "clean though poor inn" and was collared by a local law enforcer who could not understand how his passport had remained unstamped. What the "gendarme" had failed to realize was that John had crossed the Simplon in a far from usual manner. It soon transpired that the officer was less interested in the appropriate paperwork than the fact that Polidori was a doctor who could take away the nagging pain of his toothache. At this point in his journal, without any preamble, John's thoughts segue into a curious comment which gives no clue to the mental path that led him to write: "It is useless to describe the picturesque: the best page to turn for it is the memory."

What prompted such an observation? Was he simply too weary to describe the valley surrounding the town, or was it the nineteenth-century equivalent of putting down the camera and mindfully contemplating a scene in all its detail, searing it into the memory? In our digital age, where the cost of film is no longer relevant, it is all too easy to see a place through the repeated taking of images which actually denies our own eyes the pleasure of truly seeing and being in the moment. Perhaps John, now in his father's homeland, did not need the filter of words to appreciate his surroundings. He went to bed early that night after "one of the most comfortable fireside evenings" he had experienced since leaving Geneva.

On the following morning, he shadowed the course of the Toce River running down towards Lake Maggiore. Given the natural lie of the land, the motorway takes the same route. Temporarily back on old form, he appraised his first "good-looking Italian girl" in Vagagna before taking a meal of grapes, nectarines and peaches in Ornavasso. From the banks of the lake, he rowed out to the Borromean Islands of Isola Madre and Isola Bella. The latter houses a palazzo and accompanying gardens that have played host to a roll call of the crowned heads of Europe. Despite visiting at the height of Gilberto Borromeo's affluence, Polidori was rather scornful of the design of the palace. He skipped the gardens as he thought he would view them from the upper rooms, but finally caught their magnificence from the waters, seeing their paved, stepped terraces rising geometrically in angular reminiscence of the mountains beyond.

John had planned to move on to the lakes of Lugano and Como, but was advised that he could reach Milan by water. As his feet were still troublesome from miles of walking, he decided to follow this suggestion and joined a party to Sesto Calende and onward by canal to Milan. Shakespeare made reference to this mode of travel to Lombardy's largest city in *The Two Gentlemen of Verona*. It is not our intention to question the authorial identity of the Bard of Avon, but Richard Paul Rowe, in his interesting book *The Shakespeare Guide to Italy: Then and Now*, points out that the oft-criticized supposed mistake of "sailing to Milan" was a distinct possibility given the network of canals that could take travellers to the very heart of the city. It was only in 1928 that the Naviglio Interno was converted into *terra firma*.

Travelling by canal was also a safer option being free of the bandits who would lie in wait for carriages. John describes the hazy drift of his barge through the flat lands outside the city where the plains were edged by protective rows of trees and the villas increased in prosperity as the size of the vineyards, fat with grapes, announced the proximity of his destination. He spent the night in this garden of Bacchus, sleeping by the canal and itching to enter what would prove to be the most significant city of his stay in the old country.

The boatmen guided him through an entrance gate and past a church he calls Santa Maria. The obvious candidate is Santa Maria delle Grazie, home to Da Vinci's *Last Supper*, but John's description of "all white marble, with many fine statues on the outside" does not fit with delle Grazie's unadorned red brick. He could have been referring to Santa Maria del Carmine, Santa Maria Podone, Santa Maria presso San Satiro, Santa Maria della Consolazione or even Santa Maria Incoronata; Milan's Santa Marias are almost infinite. We had less trouble with the location of his rooms in the ambiguously named "Contrado San Spirito". John, in his journal, confused the gender as it should be *contrada* which can either refer to a parcel of land, a city district, quarter or street, the latter being more commonly rendered in Italian as *via*.

Within the confines of the historic centre in what is now known as the Quadrilatero della Moda (the Fashion Quarter), we were able to locate Via Santo Spirito. The ornate baroque balconies that dress the slender multi-storey façades resonate with Polidori's explanation that he rented a second-storey apartment with a bedroom and sitting-room. The right-hand side of this one-way street must have been reconstructed; its plain, austere regularity is home to a state secondary school. As the children pour out from the twin wooden doors, they are confronted with the expensive fashions of Carlo Tivoli and, to Anglo ears, the less exotic sounding Neil Barrett.

John's first foray into the Milanese night was, of course, a solo trip to La Scala – the famous opera house which is just a short walk from the cathedral. We know that he went to see a ballet, *La Testa di Bronzo*, composed by Carlo Evasio Soliva, appropriately enough a Swiss-Italian who had only recently premiered the piece, much to the acclaim of the French writer, Stendhal, whom John would shortly meet. After the upset of leaving Byron, the solitary hike through the Alps and the aches and pains enforced by travel with little money, this taste of Italian culture was like a balm to his creative soul and led him to rhapsodize in his diary: "the ballet the most magnificent thing I ever saw".

In the following days, between further visits to the theatre and perusing the booksellers' wares, Polidori endeavoured to make or remake acquaintances. John's firmest friend in Milan would be Luigi de Brême, confusingly often referred to as Monsignor de Brême having originally trained as a priest. However, his open-minded ideas conflicted with his priestly vocation and he dropped religion in favour of a more literary and bohemian life. Polidori had already met Brême at one of Madame de Staël's soirees at Coppet, also attended by Byron. The former Monsignor was a handsome man in his early thirties who shared John's liberal politics, not to mention his appreciation of the female form.

Finding himself on an even keel, John finally felt able to write to Byron and tell him of his journey. Franklin Bishop, in his biography, *Polidori!*, is sure that the doctor's letter to his former employer, written at the beginning of October, is evidence that the relationship between the two had not been as sour as Thomas Moore had led readers to believe in his book. The tone is respectful and light, as evidenced by the following excerpt:

> My route has been throughout accompanied with the most magnificent scenery, I shall not describe any part, both because you will also, I hope, tread the same road. I have not seen the lake of Como — my left foot being out in the heel by new shoes. I have been obliged always almost to walk with it down at heel and the consequence may well be imagined — I now am of the Contrada San Spirito. — remember me kindly to Mr Hobhouse and to assure yourself that I am your Lordship's obedient and humble servant.

It seems to us that the kindly remembrance to Hobhouse is much more than Byron's friend actually deserved, being, as he was, the final catalyst for Polidori's removal.

Much talk at Brême's residence revolved around the Austrian occupation of Milan and Italian resistance to their temporary overlords. The Austrians had spies everywhere and liberals like Brême needed to be extremely careful. John had the perfect excuse, which was in fact true, that his visits were intended to help Luigi with his English. In return, Polidori received assistance in the translation of his play, *Count Orlando*. The developing friendship saw John included in the circle that would regularly gather at La Scala.

It was almost inevitable that such a gathering would attract Byron who, as John suspected in his letter, had indeed been making his way to Milan, accompanied by the fork-tongued Hobhouse. For the first time, the poet and the doctor met, if not as equals then at least on the same social playing field. If anything, Polidori had the advantage of speaking the language fluently and the friendship of the influential Brême. News of Byron's arrival swept through the city and his first appearances at the opera were greeted with gawping women who had travelled from provincial Lombardy in the hope of talking to the aristocratic seducer.

It was not only the daughters of rich landowners who went weak at the knees on meeting the poet; Marie-Henri Beyle, better known as the writer, Stendhal, was overcome with emotion when greeting his hero. It only took a few sentences for the Frenchman to be disabused of his preconceptions regarding Byron's personality. Nevertheless, it did not stop Stendhal later dining out on his largely favourable reminiscences of Byron in Milan. As regards Polidori, he found him handsome – a compliment the doctor was unable to return, describing Beyle as "a fat lascivious man".

To this welter of recollection and character analysis, we can add Hobhouse, casting Stendhal as "a little, fat, whiskered man" but describing Brême more fully as "an Abbate, one of Napoleon's almoners for the Kingdom of Italy, whence his title – the son of a noble Piedomontese family, destined for the church, who has been offered two bishoprics by Napoleon, and one by these people, but wishes to rather unfrock himself than put on the mitre". Hobhouse also considered him "one of the most attractive men I ever saw".

Byron's friend would later revise his opinions for something far more acerbic; however, for the time being, he was happy to listen attentively to Brême's discourses on the state of Italian literature. The one-time monsignor was at the heart of a coterie of writers, including Silvio Pellico, the author of the Dante inspired *Francesco da Rimini*; the poet and playwright, Vincenzo Monti; the composer, naturalist and author, Giuseppe Acerbi, and Pietro Borsieri, the writer of *Giorno*. In his voracious diary output, Hobhouse gives an account of the spat between Brême and Acerbi who were championing the Romantics and the Classicists, respectively. Acerbi held Brême to be a little too self-important, whereas the former cleric thought Acerbi's injudicious editing of an article by Madame de Staël somewhat outrageous.

Polidori was already part of this literary debate, siding with Brême and Borsieri, when Byron and Hobhouse entered the metaphorical fray. Brême considered Byron to be the most lauded poet since Petrarch; an opinion surely designed to curry favour with the Englishman. Significantly, considering John's delicate dynamic with Byron and Hobhouse, the three men decided to visit the Ambrosian Library together. The Biblioteca Ambrosiana is still to be found in the Piazza Pio XI and was instigated by Cardinal Federico Borromeo in 1609. The building has undergone several refurbishments, suffering from bomb damage in the Second World War during which it lost La Scala's libretti archives. It remains a prodigious library that contains classical, historical, literary and sacred volumes, including numerous rare codices by da Vinci, not to mention an art collection with his *Portrait of a Musician* and Caravaggio's *Basket of Fruit*.

The building, as approached from Via Cesare Cantù, has a Neoclassical façade in a colour reminiscent of a faded manuscript. The Renaissance doorway has something of the triumphal arch in its appearance being flanked by two rather plain pilasters in the Tuscan style. These days, the building is draped in the enormous wall-hangings so beloved of Italian museums which advertise the current displays on offer inside. Polidori had no need of such extravagant promotional material – he knew they would be seeing some very special artefacts:

> and the Ambrosian, where I saw the Virgil with marginal notes of Petrarch; some of the pieces of MSS. of the Plautus and Terence, fragments edited by Mai. – Some of the paintings there are beautiful. The Milanese Raphael has some heads expressing such mild heavenly meekness as is scarcely imagined.

John had the twofold joy of reading Virgil in the original, annotated by the very same Renaissance poet that his friend, Brême, had compared to Byron. He makes no mention of the most famous Raphael in the library which is the cartoon preparation for his *School of Athens*, donated by Fabio Borromeo Visconti's widow in 1626.

Byron, as usual, had his own agenda. He was drawn by the letters, verses and locks of hair exchanged between Pietro Bembo and Lucrezia Borgia, with whom she had an affair during her third marriage to Alfonso d'Este, the Duke of Ferrara. Byron elaborates in a letter to his sister, dated 15 October:

> I suppose you know that she was a famous beauty, and famous for the use she made of it; and that she was the love of this same Cardinal Bembo (besides a story about her papa Pope Alexander and her brother Caesar Borgia – which some people don't believe – and others do), and that after all she ended with being Duchess of Ferrara, and an excellent mother and wife also; so good as to be quite an example. All this may or may not be, but the hair and the letters are so beautiful that I have done nothing but pore over them, and have made the librarian promise me a copy of some of them; and I mean to get some of the hair if I can. The verses are Spanish – the letters Italian – some signed – others with a cross – but all in her own handwriting.

Of all the people Byron could have written to about Lucrezia, nobody would have understood better than his half-sister, Augusta Leigh. The mutterings of incest that surrounded Lucrezia's life would have been familiar to them both, given aspects of the scandal that prompted the poet to flee England. It was also rumoured that Byron had his own collection of female locks although not always from the lady's scalp. Whether or not he managed to attain some of the Duchess of Ferrara's hair is open to question, but he did boast elsewhere that he had possession of such a prize.

Hobhouse is much more pragmatic in his account, enumerating the exhibits he saw and stressing his disgust at how the monks abused manuscripts of Cicero's works by scrawling their missals across his words. However, it is thanks to Hobhouse that we have a description of the theatre, La Scala: "a magnificent house, divided into six circles of boxes and a large pit, the back of which is an open space for walking . . . The orchestra very roomy – the whole theatre larger than any in London, I think." The opera house was, without doubt, a place of reunion for Brême's circle. It would also prove to be the site of Polidori's undoing. Just as John had found a home in Milan and friends with whom he could share his love of literature and his medical training, our doctor once more decided to press the self-destruct button.

During his weeks in the city, John had been steeped in the rhetoric of Italian independence, mixing with people who resented the Austrians' presence. On the evening of 28 October, Polidori entered La Scala with his friend, Borsieri, and Hobhouse. On spotting an Austrian soldier still wearing his hat, thus blocking the view, John's hackles rose in reckless indignation and, full of pointless braggadocio, he asked the grenadier to remove the offending headwear. Hobhouse picks up the story:

> The Captain, who was the officer on guard, turned round and said, "Vorrete?" — "Io voglio", returned Polidori — the officer desired him to step out with him. Polidori called me to come out with him, thinking he was to fight, but was soon undeceived by being ordered into the custody of two grenadiers into the guard-house.

The captain's Italian "'Vorrete?'" simply means "You wish me to?", but would perhaps be better interpreted as "You really think I'm going to do that?" Polidori's response creates a stand-off between the two; the situation was worsened still further by the fact that the grenadier was the officer charged with keeping order in the theatre and, as such, was required to wear his hat.

Polidori, in elegant Italian, persisted in his refusal to co-operate, which was met with a barrage of Teutonic swearing that John calls "Billingsgate German". Ever concerned with status, Polidori told the officer that he was every bit his equal, to which came the reply, noted by Hobhouse, that he was a "'Verfluchter kerl'" ("accursed cove") who was not even equal to the meanest soldier. Matters now started to spiral out of control and a plethora of assorted friends and acquaintances amassed in the guardhouse which was also now full of soldiers.

Byron felt obliged to join the melee and a curious Stendhal tagged along like a rubber-necking bystander at a traffic accident. The Frenchman describes what happened next: "There were fifteen or twenty of us gathered around the prisoner. Everybody was talking at once. M. Polidori was beside himself and red as a beet. Lord Byron, who on the contrary was very pale, was having great difficulty in containing his rage." Stendhal also claimed that it was the composer, Monti, who shouted the following: "'Sortiamo tutti, restino solamente i titolati'" ("Everybody out, except those with titles"). Whoever may have said this, it had the desired effect, leaving Byron and Brême, with Byron giving his card to the Austrians by way of guarantee that Polidori would appear the day after to account for his actions.

John's friend, Brême, tried every conceivable plea to ensure matters were not taken any further but to no avail. The most detailed description of what happened next comes from Polidori, himself:

> Next morning I received a printed order from the police to attend. As soon as I saw the order I went to De Brême, who accompanied me to the gate. I entered. 'Where do you wish your passport viséd for?' 'I am not thinking of going.' 'You must be off in four-and-twenty hours for Florence.' 'But I wish for more time.' 'You must be off in that time, or you will have some-thing disagreeable happen to you.'

Brême, once more, went to appeal to other authorities and John fell back on the kindness of his former employer, Byron, and nemesis, Hobhouse. To their credit, they both appealed his expulsion but the matter had already been decided. Despite Polidori's foolishness, the Austrians were not entirely blameless; there were many instances of the brutish behaviour of their soldiers, who brooked no insubordination from the Italians.

John left Milan, broken-hearted to be leaving his dear friend, Brême, weeping "in his arms like a child, for his kindness and friendship". As a thunderstorm broke, the virtually penniless doctor made his way to Lodi, hoping that an uprising would occur so he could fight the hated occupiers. Not for the first time on this odyssey to the land of his fore-bears, Polidori trudged away, dejected and in tears.

A strange codicil to this incident can be found in Hobhouse's diary, superbly curated by the late Peter Cochran. The day after John's departure, Hobhouse and Byron were called upon by Brême and, in his journal, Hobhouse recalls that "we foolishly argued Polidori's case till we told the truth about the man and might do him mischief". Cochran adds a footnote at this point explaining that the truth they purported to reveal was John's homosexuality. There have been analyses of *The Vampyre* that see the relationship between the two male protagonists as a sexual metaphor, but nowhere else in our research have we ever encountered a reference to John being gay. The supposed smear would matter little in our more enlightened times but, in the Georgian era, it would have been of great consequence. Was this an attempt by Hobhouse to create trouble for John? It also seems incredibly hypo-critical of the pair in the light of Byron's more than passing acquaintance with the love that dare not speak its name. Interestingly, Paul West, in his raucously lewd fictionalization of the journey, has Polidori often dampening the ardour of a rapacious Byron.

From Lodi, John fell in with a Prussian who had been expelled from Heidelberg for slapping a Russian. The two must have had much to talk about and they were afforded the opportunity as they shared a coach and subsequently a room at an inn in Casalpusterlengo. This was but a fleeting stop on the way to Parma, the dairy capital of Reggio Emilia. We approached Parma with sighs of relief having been stuck for far too long on the Milanese ring road, enormously grateful for the soothing hum of the car's air-conditioning.

Our only previous visit to Parma was via the television, guided by the gloriously cavalier gourmand, Keith Floyd. Floyd had staged a cookery sketch in the Piazza del Duomo, attempting to demonstrate veal in a cream sauce. With the rain beginning to lash down in an empty square, umbrellas had to be opened, prompting the chef to resort to his customary "slurp" of the local wine whilst haranguing the poor soundman for the noises off created by the splashing rain. It was with surprise that we walked into an equally empty square in much more clement weather. Had this been Florence, we would not have been able to walk in a straight line between the Baptistery and the Duomo, but we had the cobbles to ourselves.

The Baptistery is an octagonal pink marble construction adorned with galleries on four levels overlooking the square. The possible architect,

Benedetto Antelami, definitely completed the reliefs in the interior of the building, in addition to the bas-relief, *Descent from the Cross*, inside the neighbouring cathedral. We were, however, more drawn to the transcendental *Assumption of the Virgin* disappearing into the illusion of the heavens on the underside of the dome. The creator of this *trompe l'oeil* masterpiece, completed in 1530, was Antonio da Correggio, who paved the way for a style known as *sotto in su*, which sounds far more romantic than the prosaic "below upward".

John gives a brief mention to both of these buildings but is clearly more concerned about his books. He was forced to leave nearly 300 volumes in the care of Brême back in Milan – a figure that constituted what little wealth he possessed. He even admitted that he was extremely unlikely to read them all. Consequently, he headed straight for a bookshop in Parma and bought Boccaccio's *Elegia di Madonna Fiammetta*. Like good little disciples, we sought out Fiaccadori, the wonderfully atmospheric bookshop on Strada Duomo, a few convenient steps from the cathedral and bought the very same.

Turning to the back cover of our Mursia edition, we discovered the story, previously only being familiar with Boccaccio's masterwork, *The Decameron*. Fiammetta is a Neapolitan noblewoman trapped in a marriage of convenience who had fallen for the charms of a Florentine merchant, Panfilo. It is the age-old tale of love and abandonment, but written in a style that was very innovative for the time. Boccaccio adopted a first-person narrative, letting Fiammetta tell her story in a plaintive novel that is "lirica e balata", lyrical and ballad-like.

Boccaccio is contemporary with Chaucer and his *Decameron* has much in common with *The Canterbury Tales*, but the two languages have taken very different evolutionary courses. A twenty-first century Italian picking up *La Fiammetta* would have little difficulty in reading a text that is over 600 years old. Of course, there is specific vocabulary and subtle shifts in meaning but witness the difference between "ultima speranza della mia mente . . . " ("my mind's last hope . . . ") and "I knowe ynogh, on even and a-morwe" ("I know enough, in the evening and the morn").

The pair also shared an earthy sense of humour. One episode of *The

Decameron has a supposedly deaf-mute gardener working in a convent and obligingly deflowering the eager nuns. Chaucer is equally scathing of the abuses of ecclesiastical power. These lines from *The Summoner's Tale* – "And in his ers they crepten everychon. / He clapte his tayl agayn and lay ful stille" – describe the devil's arse (ers), the hiding place for many a friar in the pits of hell.

With his book tucked under his arm, Polidori mounted a carriage for Bologna, still accompanied by the Russian-slapping Prussian. He sped through Reggio, over-nighting in Rubiera, before admiring the Ghirlandina tower of Modena. The customs officers at Modena took a dislike to his luggage and were going to send it for further investigation, chiefly due to the sensitive nature of some of his books. On invoking the magic word, "physician", he was allowed to pass, the officers knowing full well they had neither the knowledge nor experience to question the texts.

Bologna, as is so often quoted in tourist guides, is the city known as the *dotta*, the *grassa* and the *rossa* (the wise, the fat and the red). Its reputation comes from its university, considered to be the first in Europe; its rich and justly-famed cuisine, and its red roofs or, as the twentieth century has proved, its left-leaning politics. Of these facets of Bolognese society, John was most concerned with its academic and ecclesiastical aspects, touring the city's churches and finding his way to the public cemetery which had only been instituted in 1801.

The cemetery is located just outside the city walls and a good three-quarters of an hour walk from the central Piazza Maggiore. San Girolamo della Certosa, to give the establishment its full name, used to be a Carthusian monastery and, in the 1810s, was rapidly becoming a stop for the grand tourist. On the heels of Polidori would follow Byron himself, as well as Stendhal and Dickens. John, ever-obsessed with the shadows of death, gives us this evocative vignette of his experience:

> Saw a coffin, when dark, brought into the church with torches. The poor are separated from the rich, and have only the turf upon them: the rich groan under the weight of marble. The priests, monks, nuns, etc., all in separate squares; a cardinal's hat covering a death's head.

One site John really should have visited is the Archiginnasio, situated in what is now known as the Piazza Luigi Galvani. As we know, Galvani and his experiments in the reanimation of frogs' legs via electrical stimulation featured in Mary Shelley's introduction to *Frankenstein*. The gathering at Diodati would have discussed such experiments. Galvani knew the Archiginnasio well owing to his appointment in theoretical anatomy at the city's Academy of Sciences.

As we walked from the Piazza Maggiore along Via dell'Archiginnasio, Galvani came into view, suitably elevated on a plinth, mid-lecture, his eyes intent on the book he is holding, one hand animated in oratory. He faces the Archiginnasio and we too, turned towards the famed Anatomical Theatre. Inside, is a heart-stoppingly evocative restoration of the 1636 room intended for surgical demonstration. From the rubble of a Second World War bomb, the Bolognese have created a beautiful recreation of the original and the room, once intended for the work of functional science, is, itself, a work of art.

Entirely clad in soft, gently worn, golden pine, the lecture hall resembles a three-tiered miniature amphitheatre. At regular intervals along the walls are carved statues of the greats of medicine that look down upon the central marble demonstration slab where cadavers would have been dissected. The slab is appropriately interred within the confines of a coffin-shaped balustrade. Polidori would have been familiar with the homilies issuing from the professors who confidently sliced the delicate tissues of the poor unfortunates they had obtained from the gallows or a pauper's grave.

Sadly for him and for us, John never visited the site and we are therefore deprived of the impressions he could have set down in his diary. Back in the less claustrophobic air of the living, the sumptuous reddish glow of the city's architecture at dusk had brought out the populace for the *passeggiata*, the tradition across the Mediterranean of walking, talking and being seen that is simply not described adequately by the English translation, 'stroll'. The perfectly designed porticoes of the city are extensive, allowing protection from winter rain and summer sun. The symmetrical elegance of these walkways is further enhanced by the depth of shadow falling from the smooth pillars and striating the paving. Suitably celebrated and often protected, you would not now expect to see the 'For Sale' signs observed by Polidori.

John was delayed in his exit from Bologna by a dispute with the Prussian. According to the coachman, our doctor had hindered his companion's departure by failing to provide security of payment. Much against his wishes, John offered a promissory note agreeing to pay for travel on arrival in Florence if the Prussian failed to do so. They eventually left on 6 November, being frustrated by buffeting winds and mist. Polidori walked the final few miles to Florence, entering the city through the Porta San Gallo.

The weight of expectation can sometimes detract from one's initial impressions of a city so eulogized that it is impossible for it to live up to its hype. This was not the first time we had visited Florence but we must confess that our initial forays, years in the past, were blighted by these burdensome preconceptions. Not the fault of the city itself but rather its position as a victim of its own success, Florence can occasionally leave a visitor expecting more than perhaps it is willing to give. Such was Polidori's own impression, as he notes down that "Florence, on entering, disappointed me . . . " Admittedly, John had to take a detour due to road repairs and therefore did not enter in the most memorable of manners.

The hypocrisy of complaining about tourist numbers is not lost on us, but it is the sheer weight of visitors that can leave one frustrated and overwhelmed. We experienced the inverse of Stendhal syndrome, who described his visit to the city in these giddy terms: "I was in a sort of ecstasy, from the idea of being in Florence, close to the great men whose tombs I had seen." It is difficult to approach anything resembling ecstasy when you are trying to view Botticelli's *Birth of Venus* through the armpit of an over-excited Texan.

We had to wise up and on this visit we left it until an hour before closing to visit the Uffizi. Not much time, we grant you, but the pleasure of having halls virtually to ourselves was worth the time limitation. John also saw the *Venus* but was more concerned in making contacts. His friend, Brême, had given him a letter of introduction to Louise of Stolberg-Gedern, more usually known as the Countess of

Albany. Louise, as we know, had been living with Alfieri, Gaetano's former employer. After the writer's death, she stayed on in Florence where she established a *salon*. We can see from Brême's letter, translated by Franklin Bishop, the esteem in which he held John:

> You would not have forgiven me had I not given a letter for you Madam, to M. Polidori, spirited and knowledgeable young man with whom I have been friendly since my trip to Switzerland. He's an Anglo-Italian whose father without a doubt has the honour of being known to you as he was the secretary of our Count Alfieri.

Brême continues by imploring the countess to aid Polidori in his search for help from British government representatives in the city. It was all in vain, though, as we can see in these words John subsequently wrote to Byron when in Pisa: "I was thinking of settling in Florence but the only person who could be of use the Countess of Albany is engaged to a French physician who cures especially her Cytherean complaints."

John felt he had no choice but to head for Arezzo where his uncle resided. Broke and travelling light, "with a shirt in my pocket", Polidori walked the distance to the town. He was accompanied by his dog, which we assume to be the same stray that had eaten something poisonous in Thun. He achieved forty-five miles in twelve hours, a pace that left his dog on the point of collapse. So intent was Polidori on reaching his destination, he failed to notice his poor companion's distress. His arrival at Luigi Polidori's house created something of a stir, with the maid flying up the stairs to find the mistress and master of the house who John describes, respectively, as "a tall, stout, slovenly woman" and "a tall, stout, handsome, mild-looking man".

It seems that John refused to divulge the state he was really in, either to his uncle or his father, to whom he wrote a letter detailing his experiences since Switzerland. There is no mention of the debacle in Milan and only vague allusions to the trouble he might be causing in terms of worry and lack of finance. He does, however, ask his father for the cost of a fare to London from Livorno, but also alludes to the fact that he was hoping for employment with Lady Westmorland in Rome.

The following year, after being informed of Polidori's failed attempts at gaining work, Byron wrote this deliciously wicked letter to Hobhouse, both satirizing the doctor's inability to cure his patients and his lack of success with the ladies: "He seems to have no luck unless he has had any with the Lady Westmorland's clitoris – which is supposed to be of the longest. I have advised him to marry if only to fill up the gap which he has already made in the population."

Uncle Luigi saw little resemblance between John and his brother, but was more upbeat about his prospects than Byron ever was: "But I think I have already discerned that the disposition of the young man is excellent, and that he will secure honour and fortune in that part of the world where good qualities count for something." This is clearly in praise of his nephew but the location of that "part of the world" is unclear – perhaps England, an Italian city or some enclave of goodly people that would benefit from his medical training, irrespective of nationality.

The only reference to the Polidori family name we were able to find in Arezzo was a street called Via Vincenzo Polidori, a quiet suburban avenue populated with modern red-brick flats and two-storey houses. We found no trace of Luigi's residence. Polidori stayed with his uncle for the best part of a week, playing cards, reading and sightseeing. Still reluctant to importune his relatives for ready cash, he left with just half a scudo in his pocket. Almost inevitably, and sadly, he lost his dog at Montevarchi. He struggled on, limping, until he reached Figline, both of which John misspelt in his diary. He resigned himself to coach transport, despite his lack of money.

The friend he had made in Geneva, Lloyd, with whom he had crashed into a horse and cart, was waiting for him in Florence. Unfortunately, he was only able to offer John twenty scudi having lost his own purse on the journey from Venice. Lloyd and other British acquaintances urged him to set up as a physician to the considerable English community in the city, but John's mind was made up. He was to go in search of Andrea Vaccà Berlinghieri, praised in John's earshot as the "*Dio della Medicina*" ("God of Medicine"), who lived in Pisa.

Contrary to popular imagination, Pisa does not centre on its leaning tower. The city's great mansions line the Lungarno, the stretch of river-front that bisects the settlement. It was along this sweep of gentrified promenade that Shelley and subsequently, Byron, set up residences in 1820 and 1821 respectively, long after John had left. The Shelleys settled in the Casa Frassi, a spacious apartment that afforded Percy the luxury of his own study and a considerable break from their itinerant lifestyle. Byron took the altogether more ostentatious Palazzo Lanfranchi-Toscanelli, a three-storeyed Renaissance palace with a porticoed entrance topped by an ornate balcony. It is often confused with its similar relative on the opposite bank of the Arno.

The confusion arises from the fact that the Toscanelli family only acquired the palace in 1827, hence when Byron settled in Pisa, there were two Palazzi Lanfranchi – the white marble palace he rented and the red-brick cousin on the Galileo Galilei side of the river. Byron even had his own boat dock, a luxury now impossible owing to the tarmacked frontage and low-slung walls built to contain the river's flow. It is on one of these walls that we noticed a plaque bearing a quote from Giacomo Leopardi, Italy's foremost Romantic poet and a contemporary of his English brethren: "L'aspetto di Pisa mi piace assai più di quel di Firenze. Questo Lung'arno è uno spettacolo così ampio, così magnifico, così gaio, così ridente, che innamora . . . " ("The appearance of Pisa appeals to me a great deal more than that of Florence. This enchanting Lung'arno is such a broad sight, so magnificent, so bright, so delightful . . . ")

Leopardi's words echo down the generations, only losing a little of their enchantment through the encroachment of the more prosaic aspects of modern-day transport. The river used to be the principal way of entering the city, whether from central Tuscany or from the sea, a short twenty-minute drive away through the now protected Parco naturale Migliarino San Rossore Massaciuccoli. Polidori came from the Florence direction after being stopped from boarding a boat in the city when the gate-officer recognized his accent as not being *"originario Toscano"*. He had to resort to an acquaintance who wrote him a declaration allowing him to travel.

One of John's first tasks in Pisa was to copy out his grandfather's *Osteologia ,* most likely as an homage to his illustrious relative, a once-respected medical figure. It was also not long before he searched out the fabled Vaccà at the hospital. Polidori was overwhelmed by the doctor's gracious welcome and the fact that the doors to his house were thrown wide in an open invitation to dinner whenever John felt the inclination. He soon settled in to a routine of visits to the hospital, study at the library and dinner at Vaccà's residence. It was inevitable that eating with such an eminent figure would bring with it introductions to the great and good of Pisan society.

John's diary is full of name-dropping at this point; from evenings with the Countess Mastrani to after dinner talk with Corsi, the lawyer, and theatre visits where he and Vaccà mixed with the Prince of Villafranca and the Countess Castelfiel. However, he had now developed a more jaundiced eye on the superficialities of high society, particularly the provincial Tuscan variety through which he now moved, not to mention the vagaries of the English aristocracy. He had obviously discussed Byron's high-handed and sarcastic demeanour with his uncle Luigi. Polidori's letter to his father from Arezzo is reproduced in *The Vampyre and other writings*. Franklin Bishop, the editor, tells us that Luigi appended these words: "I became indignant at some references to the strange conduct of that Lord Byron with whom he was travelling: but he kept his temper well – I envy him for that. All these people are hard: Patience!"

Luigi was only hearing one side of the story and we know John had his tantrums, but the discussion and his subsequent observations on the icy salon of Countess Mastrani are enough to suggest that the scales had well and truly fallen from Polidori's eyes. One of the last and most poignant entries in his diary comes from Boxing Day 1816. He accompanied Vaccà on a trip to Livorno or Leghorn, as John and the local English community referred to it. Livorno was, and still is, a considerable port with, in the nineteenth century, regular connections to England. John made for the sea and "stood gazing some time on the waves".

Polidori was looking into a future that still refused to reveal itself. His uncertainties are exposed in letters he wrote to Byron in January of the following year. Firstly, he reveals the extent to which Vaccà was influencing his medical advancement:

I thought myself very free from medical prejudice but by his instruction by his demonstration of how much is thought fact in medicine which is merely a rash induction. My presumption is much diminished & I have put myself to study again what I thought I knew. I divide my time between the hospital reading medicine & Italian literature till 4 when I dine with him & afterwards accompany his wife to the theatre . . .

We already know of Byron's later scathing aside to Hobhouse regarding John's medical skills; therefore this letter must have raised a sardonic eyebrow. Polidori continues by revealing his plan of employment with Lady Westmorland in Rome and of a somewhat madcap scheme to act as a physician to the expat Danish community in Brazil, a contact that he had received through Olindo Giusto, a friend of Vaccà's. A further insight into John's troubled mind comes from the subsequent letter to his Lordship:

I have arranged the observations I have made upon different subjects in Italy but especially medicine & surgery into the shape of a journal and I think I have got some interesting information upon the state of these last two sciences and I have at least in my own eyes put it upon paper in if not an accurate at least a clear style might I ask your Lordship to recommend to Murray[?] I have also a play, *The Duke of Athens,* but I fear at this you will be more inclined to laugh than any thing else, but as I wish to go to the Brazil and I do not think my father will help me, might I ask your Lordship to read & judge it.

Polidori then proceeds to ask Byron if he could afford him an introduction to some English people who have influence at the Portuguese court and stresses his anxiousness about the Brazil plan. Both the medical treatise and the play seemed designed to generate enough money to allow him to emigrate and start a new life. Byron could have so easily dismissed these letters with a wave of the hand, yet it is to the poet's credit that he actually contacted his publisher and recommended Polidori's medical writings: "he is clever – and accomplished – and is honourable in his dealings – and not at all malevolent. He has kept a journal under the eye of Vaccà at Pisa – Vaccà has corrected it – and it must contain some valuable hints or information on the practise of this Country."

It is unclear to what extent John was ever paid for his hospital work with Vaccà and his proffered publications came to nothing. Polidori's only profitable employment in Pisa came from the English expatriate community, notable amongst whom was Francis North, the Earl of Guilford. Unfortunately for Polidori, when he took on his clients, they were all seriously ill with little hope of recovery, and therefore liable to die under his care. During this period of his life, rather than being remembered for the copious medical essays that should have been published, he became notorious in Romantic circles as the man who killed all his patients.

Another possible patient was Francis Horner, a founder of the *Edinburgh Review* and an MP of liberal inclination. It is an indication of his state of health that Horner came to Pisa, explicitly for its climate in much the same way that Keats sought out warmer climes. D. L. Macdonald points out that Francis' brother claimed Vaccà had been his only physician and that Polidori was only called in to consult when the unfortunate man was virtually dead. Vaccà's autopsy revealed "enlargement of the air cells" for which there was no cure.

In a similar manner, uncertainty surrounds Polidori's treatment of Charles Hope, the son of collector and novelist, Thomas Hope. It seems that Hope Jnr fell ill in Pisa in December and was attended by numerous physicians from the vicinity. John may have been one of them. Macdonald even suggests that Polidori could have travelled with the family to Rome as their doctor, given that Charles died in the city. However, there are no letters or journal entries to verify this possibility. Nevertheless, Polidori did visit Rome and left his impressions in the text that accompanied Bridgens' *Costumes of Italy, Switzerland and France.*

On one page, Bridgens drew a funeral procession with a hooded penitent holding a pole displaying a fabric representation of the Virgin and Christ. Polidori added this annotation:

The show and pomp of a funeral is not the most insignificant of those many ceremonies which rivet the strangers' attention in Rome. The crossed hands, the bare feet, the placid features of the corpse dressed out in all the finery of its rank, the low chanting of the dirge, the humble pacing of the sandalled monks, of the white masked penitents bearing tapers in their hands, the pompous stately march of the richly dressed priests, form a most magnificent and melancholy spectacle.

This degree of detail is clearly from first-hand experience. It was in Rome that John also finally met with Lady Westmorland. At the age of seventeen, Jane Huck-Saunders became the second wife of John Fane, the forty-one year old Earl of Westmorland. In 1810, the couple went their separate ways. Byron had first met Jane in Algeciras in Southern Spain during his first trip abroad and was convinced that she, somewhat satirically, conceived of him as a barbarian. Lady Jane went on to carve out a niche for herself as the foremost English expat in Rome. Prior to departure from Britain, she had already conducted a series of affairs with men of her own age.

In 1817 she would have been thirty-five and in her prime at the centre of Roman intrigue. Years later, Joseph Severn, the artist friend of the ill-fated John Keats, noted the impact he had made on her and the effect she had on men younger than herself. Peter Koch, a biographer of the proto-archaeologist, Frederick Catherwood, claims that Severn suggested Catherwood as a replacement for him on an expedition to Egypt with Lady Westmorland. Severn recalled Catherwood being utterly smitten and stumbling for words at this opportunity. He would become her lover and eventually take up residence in her palazzo.

Given the obvious physical attractions of our youthful Polidori, it is safe to assume that Jane Huck-Saunders would have been delighted to have him close at hand, using his medical background as a pretext for more amorous intentions. There is no evidence of a relationship between the two, although Polidori biographer, Macdonald, suggests the high probability of John working as her physician. Once again, we turn to Byron for gossipy confirmation of John travelling with Lady Westmorland: "He travelled to Florence with the Sapphic Westmoreland – and that black sheep – Mrs George Lamb – and thence with the as yet unembowelled Lord G., Lady G., and a Miss Somebody . . ."

The references to Lord and Lady G concern the Guildfords, specifically the couple who inherited the titles from the now-deceased Francis North. Frederick North, the new fifth Earl of Guilford, was travelling back to England via Venice and John accompanied him and his wife. The mention of Lord G's "unembowelled" status is a sarcastic allusion to John's surgical removal of the former Earl's bowels for shipment to Britain. Byron elucidates in this letter to Thomas Moore dated April 1817:

> Lord Guilford died of an inflammation of the bowels: so he (Polidori) took them out, and sent them (on account of their discrepancies) separately from the carcass, to England. Conceive a man going one way, and his intestines another and his immortal soul a third! Was there ever such a distribution?

Aside from the amusement this afforded Byron, the statement carries an unforeseen weight. After he died of fever in the malarial swamps of Missolonghi, waiting to fight the Turks in a bid for Greek independence, Byron's lungs remained in the town whilst his pickled remains were shipped to the United Kingdom. Goodness only knows in which direction his immortal soul headed.

When Polidori arrived in Venice, Byron had been resident there since 10 November, the date on which the poet, accompanied by Hobhouse, had been rowed across the lagoon from Mestre in a gondola, a mode of transport that he memorably described in the following manner: "It glides along the water looking blackly, / Just like a coffin clapt in a canoe, / Where none can make out what you say or do . . . "

This clearly alludes to the assignations that took place in covered gondolas. Venice, at the time, was a city in decay, ruled by the Austrians and home to all manner of licentious behaviour. Carnival had turned into a lifestyle, fuelled by a disproportionately high percentage of courtesans and aristocratic riff-raff. Initially, Byron shunned the ostentatious palazzi of the Grand Canal and took rooms off the Frezzeria, a labyrinthine alley just to the west of Piazza San Marco.

We did not have the luxury of a gondola entry into Venice, a mode of transport now confined to rich North Americans and Japanese. Instead, we trundled across the rail bridge, likened by the writer Tiziano Scarpa, to a fishing line that has caught the Venetian fish. We, too, ignored the Grand Canal, and went in search of what remains of the Frezzeria, being surprised by the preservation of the street plan. The district is still a mercantile area, although trade is now reliant on tourism, as is the city as a whole. It often seems that the sheer weight of people is responsible for the city sinking into the mud. The situation has become so desperate that it has awakened the UNESCO giant who, at the time of writing, has threatened Venice with 'at risk' blacklisting if measures are not taken to restrict numbers. Consequently, the council have been discussing ticketed entry to St Mark's Square and other overcrowded sites, such as the waterfront known as the Riva degli Schiavoni.

Byron's original accommodation is rather more off the beaten track, although it is impossible to escape the awnings and umbrellas of shops and cafes. The poet's lodgings were in the Piscina di Frezzeria and take some seeking out amongst the seemingly identical narrow façades with grilled windows and peeling plaster. A small number indicating house 1673 is the giveaway but there is no commemoratory plaque, simply a firmly bolted metal door presenting an impassive face to the world. The building used to be a linen drapers run by the Segatis. Had Polidori accompanied him at the time, he would have doubtless said that Milord "fell like a thunderbolt" on the draper's attractive wife.

Marianna Segati, however, was no passive chambermaid but a fiery woman of passion who was happy to take advantage of the convention that allowed a married woman to take a *cicisbeo* or *cavalier servente*, that is to say, a lover tacitly accepted by the husband. In fact, these two terms are a little aristocratic for Marianna; Byron would more probably have been an *amoroso*. The family, though, were successful in business and Signor Segati was not above taking his own lovers. In his own words, Byron describes to Thomas Moore, the delights of his new conquest:

> I have got some extremely good apartments in the house of a 'Merchant of Venice', who is a good deal occupied with business and has a wife in her twenty-second year. Marianna [Segati] (that is her name) is in her appearance altogether like an antelope. She has the large, black, oriental eyes, with that peculiar expression in them which is seen rarely among Europeans – even the Italians

— and which many of the Turkish women give themselves by tinging the eyelid, — an art not known out of that country, I believe.

It was the eyes, her luscious dark locks and beautiful voice that hooked Byron, not to mention her lack of English convention and politesse. Evidence of her possessive feelings for the poet comes from another of his letters to Moore. One evening, Byron was alone in the house when a nineteen year old woman came to visit, saying she was Marianna's sister-in-law. The aristocrat claimed they were making polite chit-chat when Signora Segati returned. After a curtesy to her relative, she proceeded to grab the young woman by the hair and repeatedly slap her around the face. As the sister-in-law fled, it was all he could do to prevent his *amorosa* from running after her. This was but one more incident to feed the Byron legend, especially as the offended relative began spreading the story around the city. To the Venetians, it was little more than an amusing anecdote but it had the English spluttering into their teacups.

Whilst in Rome, Polidori had been pressed for information about Byron and had doubtless passed on some of the salacious aspects that the poet would have preferred to remain private. When the two met in Venice on 10 April, John conveyed to his former employer the kind of gossip that was doing the rounds further south which, according to a letter Byron wrote to his friend, Scrope Davies, included "a parcel of rumours . . . about harlotry women". Byron had forewarning of Polidori's visit from Hobhouse and was dismayed to find out that the doctor would be accompanying the new Lord Guilford — a man he despised enough to call the worst of "perambulating humbuggerers". In the aforementioned Scrope Davies letter, the poet went on to have tremendous fun at the expense of both his former physician and the detested Guilford family.

The doctor Polidori is here on his way to England with the present Lord Guilford — having actually embowelled the last at Pisa and spiced and pickled him for his rancid ancestors. The said Doctor has had several (patients) invalids under his prescriptions but now has no more patients — because his patients are no more — the following is the Gazette Extraordinary according to his last despatches – Lord Guilford – killed – inflammation of the bowels. Mr Horner – killed – diseased lungs. Mr Thomas Hope's son killed – scarlet fever. Rank and file – killed – 45 paupers of Pisa – wounded and missing (the last supposed to be dissected) 18 in the hospitals of that city. Wounded Lady Westmorland – incurable – her disease not defined.

It is difficult to read this without laughing but, as we know, it would have cut Polidori to the quick. The reference to Lady Westmorland refers to her sexual voraciousness as being "incurable" and we know from further letters that Byron considered it was a missed opportunity for John that he had not become her more permanent doctor and lover.

John was entrusted with two miniature portraits intended for Byron's half-sister and he was instructed to deliver them to John Murray, Byron's publisher. In a letter to Murray, several months later, the poet hopes the said portraits were delivered by the doctor and his former recommendation that Murray assist Polidori in publishing his works is given a far more sardonic twist. In the intervening period, John had submitted a verse drama, prompting Byron to write a mocking refusal that Murray could send to the would-be playwright:

> Dear Doctor, – I have read your play
> Which is a good one in its way,
> Purges the eyes, and moves the bowels,
> And drenches handkerchiefs like towels . . .
> But – and I grieve to speak it – plays –
> Are drugs – mere drugs, Sir, nowadays . . .
> There's Byron's too who once did better . . .
> So alter'd since last year his pen is,
> I think he's lost his wits at Venice.

This is typical of Byron who could give with one hand and take with the other. John was to know nothing of these satirical barbs and whilst he was in Venice, he visited Byron every day, perhaps under the illusion that he had gained some respect in the aristocrat's eyes. Indeed, Byron thought him "improved in manner" but, as he told Hobhouse, somewhat drunk on the company he had been keeping.

Never his forte, Polidori was nevertheless moved to write a poem on leaving Italy. The sonnet evokes the landscape and his feelings of remorse at returning to a land where he felt both at home and a foreigner: "So have I left Ausonia's wanton strand, / In search of thee, though barren still, my native land." John returned to London as Guildford's travelling physician. The party made their way through central France and crossed the Channel to the town where Polidori first felt the sting of Byron's wit. The April of 1817 was the last time John was to see Italy and Lord Byron.

CHAPTER SIX

The Return
Dippel's Acid

It must have been with a strong mix of emotions that Polidori knocked on the front door of his parent's home in Great Pulteney Street in London's Soho. As the first weak sunshine of early summer approached, Gaetano and his family ushered the lost wanderer back into the fold. He would have been looking forward to seeing his sister, Frances, with whom he had always had a close relationship, but she had taken up a post as a governess in the Home Counties. The only siblings he found at home were his two young sisters, who were not old enough to mitigate the post-mortem that would inevitably ensue with his father concerning the debacle of his employment with Byron.

The words 'I told you so' cannot have been far from Gaetano's lips but this would have served little purpose given the future was now more important than the past. As John suspected, his father was in no mood to support any of his more outlandish ideas and expected his son to forge a more sensible path. With no hope of immediate employment in London, he turned to Norwich. Andrew McConnell Stott tells us that, fortunately for John, his father aided him in this decision by writing to Polidori's old contacts in the city. It was suggested that John relocate in readiness for a medical position that may become available.

Consequently, Polidori made haste for East Anglia, taking lodgings in Norwich's Upper Market Place. The Square is still a vibrant warren of stalls selling everything from Asian chilli paste to rucksacks and flowers. The Guildhall also adjoins the northern fringe of the market, a clear testament to the city's mercantile history. Norwich has a long tradition of welcoming incomers including Flemish Protestants, Dutch merchants and French Huguenots fleeing persecution. The initial wave

Costessey Hall c. 1850, Costessey, photographer unknown, Wikipedia

Costessey Hall outbuildings in ruin, A. Edwards

Cover of the book,
*Costumes of Italy,
Switzerland and France*, A.
Edwards (from the British
Library collection)

The Hardy Tree,
St Pancras Old
Church, London,
A. Edwards

of immigrants in the sixteenth and seventeenth centuries would have passed through the Merchant's House, which appropriately became known as the Strangers' Hall. Many were weavers and their craftsmanship was welcome in the city.

In contrast to this swathe of Lutheran continental exiles, some of the aristocracy maintained their Catholic faith. Italians were also a common sight. Frank Meeres, in his lively account of immigrants' lives entitled *Strangers – A History of Norwich's Incomers*, tells the anecdote of a religious minister meeting two itinerant Italian artists. The well-travelled minister addressed the pair in their own language and discovered that they were originally from Florence and had walked all the way from London carrying their works on their heads. Meeres says that many of the artists who settled in Norwich were makers of figurines and hailed from Lucca. They were to find that their reproductions of saintly images and religious iconography had a limited market and, therefore, they adapted their style to local tastes. At the time of John's arrival, a certain Giuliano Crostea was operating a ring of street-sellers who wandered the alleyways of the city and the country roads of Norfolk.

Norwich was not the backwater that it may, at first, appear. Although not in London's league, it had a lively debating tradition and was open to ideas from the continent. John became an active member of the Philosophical Society and was once again taken under the wing of William Taylor. We know that Polidori was well-ensconced by July 1817 as he writes to the publisher, John Murray, asking for any reply to be sent to the city. This is the same letter in which he encloses the play that Byron cruelly mocked in verse in his own letter to Murray. It seems that the publisher had asked Byron for a way of politely declining Polidori's drama, but had instead received the spiteful rhyme. It is interesting to note that Murray thought John "not without literary talents", although writing for the theatre was not one of them.

The connection with Byron was of great help in Norwich's literary circles and provided John the means of creating interest through first-hand experience of the notorious philanderer. Having touched the coat-tails of fame, Polidori found the young ladies of the city in his thrall. He once again renewed acquaintance with the besotted

Martineau sisters and, as we know, thanks to the future novelist, Harriet, he had fallen for her elder sister. Nothing came of the friendship but he was often to be found at the Martineau home, Gurney House, in the court of the same name, just off Magdalen Street. The gated entrance allows the glimpse of two plaques – one to Elizabeth Fry, the prison reform campaigner, and the second to Harriet Martineau, which reads: "Authoress and pioneer in opening many new spheres of work for women." There is also now an annual lecture held at the playhouse in Harriet's name, instituted during the successful application process for UNESCO City of Literature status.

Now, as then, Norwich is a very literary city. The University of East Anglia is currently home to a highly influential School of Literature, Drama and Creative writing. It also provides the post-graduate course of choice in the field of literary translation. Notable alumni of the university include Ian McEwan and Kazuo Ishiguro. Printing in the city dates back to Anthony de Solempne who emigrated from Brabant in 1567. The first book to roll off Norwich's presses was, in fact, Dutch and entitled *Belijdenisse Ende* (*Confessions of Faith*).

Religion was undoubtedly one of the topics discussed at the Philosophical Society, given the area's radical background. Its members came from a variety of disciplines and were intellectuals in fields as diverse as literature, science, art and medicine; although it is as well to remember that professional specialisms were not as defined as they are today. For example, the German polymath, Goethe, distinguished himself in poetry, mineralogy, botany and drama, with side-lines in art and politics. John felt comfortable in these circles and gave talks at the society, whilst also seeking the patronage of the aristocracy.

Lady Jerningham and her husband, Sir George, were more than happy to open their doors to the doctor. Their country house was at Costessey Hall, the manor overlooking the village of the same name a few miles from his accommodation in Upper Market Place. We went in search of the residence, expecting to find a grand Elizabethan pile complete with step-gable ends topped with fluted chimneys and a turreted central tower. We were to be disillusioned. The only signs pointing us in the appropriate direction signalled the location of a golf course. With little else to guide us, we followed the gravel path to Costessey Park Golf Club and searched the horizon for clues.

Middle-aged golfers were trundling their trolleys out of the somewhat prefabricated clubhouse and down the green sward of the first fairway. In the middle-distance, two ruined chimneys protruded above some stately trees which interrupted the rough and blocked access to the putting green. Unwilling to pay the green fee for the privilege of viewing the house, we doubled back behind some newly developed flats and took a small path by an adjacent fairway. The path afforded a much better view and we were able to make out the full extent of Costessey Hall's ruin. Gothically dark against the pale blue sky, the façade had no window panes, the roof had crumbled to let in the vagaries of the weather and the chimney stacks were providing a home for the local birdlife. The golf club had fenced off the building and, within the perimeter, shrubbery had reclaimed the once tailored gardens.

As we stood observing the last of a residence that dated back to 1066, we caught the shadow of an approaching figure. A young man, dressed in wellingtons, strode purposefully towards us as we began to feign innocence. His opening gambit informed us, rather unnecessarily, that this was a golf club and, as a green keeper, he felt duty bound to tell us it was both private land and rather dangerous to stand where we were, given the dubious quality of the golfers. He was right, of course, and at any moment a stray shot from a blue-rinsed pensioner could whistle past our ears or worse. Duly chastened, we retreated whilst looking over the grounds that Polidori used to drive through on his horse-drawn gig. The dangers he encountered were not from errant golf balls but the kind of trees with their prominent gnarly roots that had blocked access to the first green.

In the September of 1817, John was driving his gig through Costessey Park when, either because of uneven ground or a startled horse, he lost control of the small carriage. We have read different accounts that state it was the gig that hit a tree, or that it was John who was thrown from his seat into the woodland. Whatever the actual details, he sustained a severe trauma to the head. Unable to move, Polidori was eventually found lying on the ground and was carried back to the manor house where he was ministered to by the staff and Lady Jerningham, herself.

He teetered on the brink of death for several days and, so gloomy was the prognosis, his family was informed.

Franklin Bishop's biography of the doctor elaborates on the extent to which he was incapacitated. It took a month for Polidori to gain a semblance of normality, although he would never be the same again. Accounts attest to a change in personality that could only be attributed to the impact that was clearly more than a mild concussion. Just as John must have been thinking that the stars were aligning to provide a more promising future, fate once again intervened to throw him off course; this time there was no hint of his usual self-sabotaging tendencies. The most telling testimony to his changed personality comes from the pen of Harriet Martineau in her autobiography, where she makes a rather stark assessment of the events: "If he had happily died then, he would have remained a hero in our imagination. The few following years (which were very possibly all the wilder for that concussion of the brain) disabused every body of all expectations of good from him."

One surprising outcome of his accident was an essay he entitled *Upon the Source of Positive Pleasure*. Lying in his recuperative bed at Costessey Hall, he drifted off to sleep and claimed he had a remarkable dream where friends from the past began to discuss the subject of pleasure. One friend, who remains unspecified, attempted to posit the argument that positive pleasure was solely dependent on the imagination and not a tangible reality. We know these were the supposed origins of his essay, as he explains the source of his ideas in the introduction. He elaborates with the following fascinating insight which appears to distance his own troubled mind from the words on the page:

> That these are the sentiments of another person I hope none will attempt to deny; for if the opinion of a certain philosopher be true, that sleep is for the convenience of souls having converse with dead or distant friends, there is not the slightest improbability in my statement. Nor can it be supposed that the experience of so young a man as myself would enable him to assert so many things in utter contradiction to all that has hitherto been felt and believed on this subject.

This introduction may well have resulted from the fact that Lady Jerningham had tactfully refused to have the essay dedicated in her name. She was neither in accord with his sentiments nor comfortable with her name being attached to the indelicate subject of pleasure. John first delivered a talk on his theory at the Philosophical Society, which must have prompted a lively debate. Despite the intended disclaimer in his preface, there is much in the essay to illustrate John's life. Speaking in the third person, Polidori gives this heartfelt summation of his own thwarted ambition:

> But he will not tell you of the profession he was studying, being one he abhorred; of the hankering he had after history, poetry, and literature, while he was obliged to study mathematics, medicine, or theology. He will not tell you how he was forced either to sacrifice his reputation, and meet disgrace before his companions, or forego the bliss of touching that more than heavenly lyre – poetry; which gives not insensate sounds, but, with its harmonious notes, breathes into vivid flames the irritable sparks of enthusiasm and hope.

At the same time as he was recuperating and mulling over these maudlin thoughts, the acrid vapours of exhausted gossip were beginning to reach him. Someone, somewhere had insinuated that Lord Byron had been less than polite about the doctor in his letters to friends. We know this from correspondence between John and the publisher, Murray, in October. The principal reason for writing was to apologize for the fact that his accident had delayed the submission of his medical journal, but it also provided an excuse for enquiring about Byron and the manner in which his Lordship should now be addressed given the gossipy reports. The trauma to John's brain would not have eased the incipient paranoia he felt regarding Byron's opinion of him. Yet, he forged on regardless, begging Murray for a copy of the poet's complete works and a piece of his handwriting.

Polidori would follow these enquiries with a further letter to Murray, submitting the medical treatise whilst damning it with his own faint praise. He doubts whether it would suit the purpose of being published in the *British Institution journal*. He also tells Murray that he now has a dispensary in Norwich thereby inferring he is still active in the medical profession. Interestingly, he signs off by saying he is thought to be well but does not feel it.

John was right to say he was not fully recovered, as his speech was becoming increasingly short and abrupt. Sentences would drift away in lost trains of thought in the manner of those suffering from aphasia. Some of the signs of faulty cerebral wiring include alterations in the inflection, stress and rhythm of his speech. It did not, however, affect the fluency of his writing, given the complexities of his essay. Unsurprisingly, the controversial subject dealt with in the text, *Upon the Source of Positive Pleasure*, was met unfavourably by the reviewers of the day.

If he had felt a bitterness at the unimaginative response of his critics, not to mention his father, a far greater storm was about to rock the already unsteady physician. By January of 1819, a deeply disillusioned John had returned to London penniless and taken rooms in Covent Garden chambers in King Street. The building still stands, although the interior has been completely gutted and refurbished. It had once been home to Sir Kenelm Digby, illustrious Catholic intellectual and privateer, who caught the wandering eye of Marie de Medici during his time on the continent. It was also a sporting and supper club which developed still further in the Victorian era.

A drawing by F. Nash in 1824, kept in the Westminster City archives, shows Covent Garden to be a chaotic maelstrom of stallholders, carts stacked with wares, itinerant hawkers and locals clamouring for the best bargains. It is a world away from the gentrified coffee shops, street performers and tourists of today. Fights were commonplace as access for carted goods was via narrow lanes, resulting in a nineteenth-century version of road-rage. Tax avoidance was so rife that, by 1830, the Earl of Bedford instituted the creation of a new market building where stalls were organized according to categories and financial contributions for selling goods could be properly administrated.

Whilst Polidori was settling in to life on the fringes of this tumult, a location completely at odds with his worsening condition, two events took place that would both enhance his mood and destroy it. The publisher, Longman, had eventually agreed to release *Count Orlando*, his dramatic tragedy, now retitled *Ximenes*. It was accompanied by *The Wreath and Other Poems*, a collection that represents the best of his few completed verses. Much to Polidori's surprise, the works had a favourable reception including a comparison with Hobhouse which left Byron's friend trailing in the doctor's wake. *The New Monthly Magazine*, however, issued a story that would turn his life upside down. Completely out of the blue, on the inauspicious date of 1 April, 1819, Henry Colburn printed *The Vampyre* with the stunning by-line, *A Tale by Lord Byron*. Polidori would have been flicking through the magazine in search of the review of *Ximenes*, but what anguish must he have felt when his eyes settled on the vampiric text. From the very first line, it would have been clear to the doctor that the work was his.

Colburn can be compared to some of the more unscrupulous members of the modern-day tabloid press, who care more about sales figures than the integrity of the text on display. He was first and foremost a man of business who had profited rather healthily from the publication of Lady Caroline Lamb's novel *Glenarvon*, the thinly disguised revenge text from Byron's former lover. He was also a purveyor of the kind of novel that gave the masses an insight into the lives of the wealthy and aristocratic, christened the "silver fork" novel by William Hazlitt.

John was incensed to find that Colburn had not only published the story in his magazine, but had also passed it on to the book publishers, Sherwood, Neely and Jones, who brought out a hardback copy a day later. Attached to the novella's appearance in the magazine, was a supposed "Extract of a Letter from Geneva" which purported to be the account of an English tourist who had gone in search of Byroniania. The letter claims the tourist had been successful thanks to the tales he had heard from Countess Breuss, stories originally recounted to her by John Polidori. John was also mentioned in the "Letter" as having penned a tale that the magazine had in its possession which they might publish in the future after talking to the author.

As Andrew McConnell Stott points out in his summation of events, this latter mention must have been a point of honour for Polidori as it suggests the magazine had been in contact with the doctor. John was quick to write to Colburn requesting some form of redress. He did not object to the appearance of *The Vampyre* but, quite rightly, said "I shall not sit patiently by and see it taken without my consent and appropriated by any person". He wanted an immediate answer and threatened Colburn with an injunction. He followed up this letter with an equally vociferous missive to Messrs Sherwood, Neely and Jones, also threatening an injunction if the book's sale was not stopped and "if the title page is not cancelled and my name inserted instead of Lord Byron".

As subsequent editions of the story came to press, Colburn simply dodged the issue by using this formula: "A tale related by Lord Byron to Doctor Polidori." Initially, Colburn had called on Polidori with a contract offering the doctor 300 pounds and an amended attribution. This seemingly fair redress was cleverly left in limbo when the slippery publisher claimed he would have this draft agreement formally written up and delivered to John. Needless to say, the contract never materialized; Colburn was mysteriously unavailable and the text continued to appear without poor Polidori receiving the appropriate credit or monies.

The Vampyre was a runaway success and was soon making appearances on the continent, both in the original language and translation. By the end of April 1819, Galignani's Paris-based magazine, Messenger, was mentioning the work and a translation quickly followed as did a German version in the following year. Johann Wolfgang von Goethe, still labouring under the misapprehension that the work was Byron's, thought it his greatest achievement. The book also crossed the Atlantic and appeared in various East Coast editions. Perhaps even more galling for the stage-struck Polidori, the French turned the piece into a play and it was performed in Paris at the Porte-Saint-Martin Theatre. These developments were to prove the tip of the iceberg as the longevity of Polidori's creation was to stretch far beyond his lifetime.

To complicate matters, the young journalist, Alaric Watts, who helped Colburn edit The New Monthly Magazine, was now trying to distance himself from the publisher's conniving duplicity. Watts had favoured a more honest approach that did not clearly state Byron to be the author and, when the tale appeared, his conscience took him to Byron's publisher, Murray, with an apology. The relationship between Colburn and his junior was rendered irreparable and Alaric resigned. Watts now cast around for someone who could shoulder the blame for his part in the debacle and he settled on Polidori, stating that John had been in contact with Colburn prior to publication. McConnell Stott also tells us that Watts claimed to be aware of John's possession of a Byron manuscript that the doctor was trying to sell. In making this assertion, the young journalist has revealed that he was not in full possession of the facts. We know from a letter written by Polidori to Murray, as far back as 1818, that John did not have the merest scrap of his illustrious former employer's handwriting.

In summation, we have an unscrupulous publisher with purely financial motives, a young employee keen to preserve his reputation, and a depressed author, stripped of his rights, who desperately needs the money. Many Byron biographers have seen Polidori's parlous situation and assumed that the imposture must be true, that John wanted the cash and was happy to ride on Byron's coat-tails in order to improve his situation. We feel this denies one fundamental truth about Polidori's life – his desire for literary status and fame, something he was never going to achieve by hiding his authorship for the sake of money. The exact truth will never be known and clearly we are championing the underdog, but not without the gathered evidence that points towards his innocence. Likewise, it will never be established how a manuscript that had been left with his friends in Geneva came to be in the avaricious hands of such a man as Colburn.

How did Byron react to *The Vampyre*? His initial response was fed by the bile that had spewed from Hobhouse's pen. This is an extract from a letter Hobhouse sent to Byron in May 1819:

> The moment, however, I saw this Vampyre, I who, like all coxcombs, know your style, swore the whole to be a vile imposture and Dolly's whole and sole doing . . . Now, however, he publishes a letter in the papers stating that though *The Vampyre* in 'its present form' is not yours, yet the 'groundwork' is 'certainly' yours. To this he put his damned Italian polysyllabic name.

Hobhouse is showing his true colours here, especially as he finishes the letter by saying, "you know I told you that you were wrong in taking him, you know I did". There is no question that Byron's friend wholly believes the scurrilous Colburn, despite the fact that he quotes Polidori who has admitted he wrote *The Vampyre* and given Byron credit for the fact that the initial idea was based on his own sketched fragment.

The differences between Byron's 'Fragment' and Polidori's fully conceived story are obvious to anyone who cares to read the two side-by-side. Perhaps to scotch the rumours for good, Byron had his text published by Murray who appended it to the poem *Mazeppa*. Famously, the poet is often quoted from his letter to Kinnaird as saying "Damn 'the Vampire', what do I know of Vampires?" He certainly did know of the legends, as his poem *The Giaour* proves. In his 'Fragment', Byron's immortal protagonist, Augustus Darvell, undertakes a journey to the ruins of Ephesus and Sardis with the narrator, where Darvell grows weak amongst the "Mahometan burial-grounds". The narrator, who in Polidori's version would become Aubrey, had already realized that Augustus was "prey to some cureless disquiet". Surrounded by the trappings of Islamic death, Darvell swears his friend to silence regarding his impending demise. When the inevitable takes place, the protagonist is buried in a shallow grave of his own choosing.

At this point, Byron's 'Fragment' ends abruptly. Polidori's tale is different, not only in style but substance. He admitted that his story includes the basic tenets of a death in the East kept secret from society but he uniquely establishes the origins of his protagonist, Lord Ruthven, as a mysterious aristocrat in London society. Aubrey does travel abroad with Ruthven to Rome, where he leaves his Lordship behind having become tired of his cruelty. Subsequently, in Greece, Aubrey develops an attachment to an innkeeper's daughter, Ianthe, who unveils the local legends of vampirism. Out walking, he is caught in a thunderstorm and looks for shelter in a hut. As he draws near, he hears the cries of a woman and a maniacal laugh. Rushing to help, he is thrown to the ground by a superhuman strength. When Aubrey comes to, he finds that Ianthe has met her end in a vampiric grasp. It is no coincidence that Ruthven makes an appearance in Athens at this point.

Once more travelling together, the pair are set upon by bandits and Ruthven is mortally wounded, yet he insists that his companion swear an oath that he will make no mention of the death for a year and a day.

Aubrey agrees and slowly returns to London, only to find that the mysterious aristocrat has reappeared in full health and is still insisting that the vow be upheld. Much to his dismay, Ruthven intends to make Aubrey's sister his bride on the very day that the oath expires. A broken Aubrey is powerless, but finally confronts his nemesis. With no means of preventing the wedding and exploding with rage, a blood vessel breaks that leads to his death. Before the inevitable happens, Aubrey is just strong enough to relate the history of Ruthven's abuse, but his guardians are too late to intervene and his sister dies, completely drained of blood.

Clearly, the fully-fleshed Polidori story is laden with original elements; yet, even if we look at that part of the tale which both texts have in common, the focus is obviously different. In this segment from Byron's 'Fragment', Darvell appears to have died:

> I felt Darvel's weight, as it were, increase upon my shoulder, and, turning to look upon his face, perceived that he was dead!
>
> I was shocked with the sudden certainty which could not be mistaken – his countenance in a few minutes became nearly black. I should have attributed so rapid a change to poison, had I not been aware that he had no opportunity of receiving it unperceived. The day was declining, the body was rapidly altering, and nothing remained but to fulfil his request . . .

Darvell's death seems poetically pre-ordained; he has arrived at a specific location to apparently die and the physicality of his demise is more graphic. However, the oath sworn by the narrator is swiftly accepted with little reluctance or anguish. By contrast, Polidori's attention settles on Ruthven's behaviour and his violent mental state. The Lord's insistence that Aubrey agree to the oath is delivered with greater urgency and passion:

> His conduct and appearance had not changed; he seemed as unconscious of pain as he had been of the objects about him: but towards the close of the last evening, his mind became apparently uneasy, and his eye often fixed upon Aubrey, who was induced to offer his assistance with more than usual earnestness . . .
>
> 'Swear!' cried the dying man, raising himself with exultant

violence, 'Swear by all your soul reveres, by all your nature dreads, swear that for a year and a day you will not impart your knowledge of my crimes or death . . . '

Interpretations of *The Vampyre* are legion. The most obvious parallel to be drawn is the relationship between Polidori and Byron for which we can substitute Aubrey and Ruthven. This description of Aubrey's character is, in part, an autobiographical sketch of the story's author: "He thought, in fine, that the dreams of poets were the realities of life." The protagonist's subsequent disillusionment also shines a light on John's disappointments during the summer of 1816:

> Attached as he was to the romance of his solitary hours, he was startled at finding, that, except in the tallow and wax candles flickering not from the presence of a ghost, but from a draught of air breaking through his golden leathered doors and felted floors, there was no foundation in real life for any of that congeries of pleasing horrors and descriptions contained in the volumes . . .

Ruthven, a name deliberately borrowed from the *Glenarvon* of Lady Caroline Lamb, had an even deeper connection to Byron's life, which is detailed fully in Franklin Bishop's biography of Polidori. As a seventeen year old, the poet saw his family's ancestral pile, Newstead Abbey, rented out to a Lord Grey de Ruthyn. It is uncertain as to whether Polidori knew this story, but Byron's former lover, Lady Caroline, would have known that Ruthyn had made a sexual advance towards the young aristocrat. Therefore, the name chosen for John's vampire is heavy with significance. His description of the character also bears a startling resemblance to his then employer. Ruthven cut a swathe through society in the same way that Byron had several years previously:

> His peculiarities caused him to be invited to every house; all wished to see him, and those who had been accustomed to violent excitement, and now felt the weight of *ennui*, were pleased at having something in their presence capable of engaging their attention. Nay more in spite of the deadly hue of his finely turned head, many of the female hunters after notoriety attempted to win his attentions, and gain, at least, some marks of what they might term affection.

Other critics have seen a homosexual subtext in both the concept of vampirism and specifically in Byron's 'Fragment' and Polidori's story. Mair Rigby, of Cardiff University, identifies the "cureless disquiet" felt by Darvell with the forbidden desire that passed between gay men. For Rigby, Ruthven is also a man wearing a mask and acting a part more acceptable to society but with coded messages for those wishing to decipher them. Aubrey could be seen as spellbound by the dominant power of Ruthven who is manipulating his latent homosexual feelings. Polidori is likely to have been unaware of the subtexts now being read into a work with the benefit of enlightened hindsight but he would have been deaf if he had not heard the rumours surrounding Byron's departure from England.

One of the most startling aspects of the entire story is Ruthven's bitter cruelty and annihilation of those in his thrall. Polidori only had recourse to fictional words on paper in conveying the true hurt he felt at the hands of a sometimes spiteful and bullying master. *The Vampyre* moves from hero worship ("He soon formed this person into the hero of a romance, and determined to observe the offspring of his fancy, rather than the individual before him") to appalled devastation ("Aubrey determined upon leaving one, whose character had not yet shown a single bright point on which to rest the eye").

The years have been kind to the genre that John created, if not to the man himself. Without the aristocratic manoeuvrings of Polidori's anti-hero, it is difficult to conceive of Count Dracula or a thousand other pale imitations of the vampire, who can move as easily through high society as he can through the Gothic crypts, castles and ruins of a moon-less night. Prior to John's invention, the vampire was a ghoul of Eastern European legend – although other cultures have laid equal claim – who rose as a rotting corpse from his unclean bed, intent on depriving the living of both their precious blood and mortal existence. Early vampires had more in common with zombies than with princes of the realm. Even Vlad the Impaler, Bram Stoker's prototype, was a tyrannical dictator rather than a darkly handsome rake.

Christopher Frayling, in his fascinating anthology, *Vampyres: Lord Byron to Count Dracula*, is one of the few to place John William Polidori in his justified position at the heart of the genre he created:

The Vampyre was the first story successfully to fuse the disparate elements of vampirism into a coherent literary genre. Polidori's style, an unusual combination (for the time) of clinical realism and weird events, was also influential, and (like the author) has been much neglected.

However much the unfortunate Polidori protested his innocence in the authorship scandal, the damage had already been done. Despite the debacle, or perhaps because of it, he managed to see *Ernestus Berchtold; or, The Modern Oedipus*, turned into print. As we know from John's travels in Switzerland, much of the content follows his own wanderings and the text is, once more, semi-autobiographical in nature. One character corrupts another and the sad protagonist unsuspectingly marries his sister. Only a handful of copies were sold, despite *The Monthly Review* claiming that it demonstrated Polidori "capable of writing in a higher and purer strain".

The black dog of depression descended further and John finally decided that it was time to turn his back on the literary world, although he continued to write in private. Rather than return to medicine, which would have been the obvious and most lucrative choice, he curiously decided to venture into the world of law. This was a bizarre scheme on two levels. Firstly, it meant expensive retraining, using money he did not possess, and secondly, his Catholic upbringing prohibited access to the upper echelons of the profession. As a Roman Catholic, he was only able to become a conveyancer of property.

Andrew McConnell Stott describes another of his strange intentions which was to join the priesthood at his *alma mater*, Ampleforth. Now far too worldly-wise for such a move, his tentative enquiry was rejected. Seeing no other alternative, he registered to train in law at Lincoln's Inn under the assumed name of John Pierce, the surname taken from his mother's maiden name. All these actions point to the making of a new start, but also to a man unable to think clearly; his brain clouded by the continuing effects of the accident in Costessey Park.

John's attempts at legal training were desultory at best, especially given that he was expected to carry out much reading and investigation without the input of a professor. In some respects, the Inns of Court were seen as a way for the gentry to finish their education, and not all who attended went on to become barristers. Compulsory dinners were commonplace where contacts could be made in the manner of a London Gentleman's Club. Polidori would have been on the lowest rungs of the hierarchy due to his religion and the lowly status of conveyancing. Given these facts, it is perhaps unsurprising that he wished to hide the further opprobrium of being known as the man who had supposedly plagiarized Byron.

It is thanks to William Michael Rossetti, Polidori's nephew, that we learn of John's move to become a lawyer and it seems that John's brother, Henry, was also a practising solicitor. Gaetano may have approved of his son's desire to shun the world of letters but would have despaired at his dabbling with another profession that would only produce benefits in the long-term. Doubtless he feared there would be more recourse to the family purse and, worse still, that of his god-father, John Deagostini, who was a some-time resident in the flat above Polidori's family home.

Unbeknownst to his father, John continued writing. Significantly, the work he was penning, *The Fall of the Angels*, first appeared, anony-mously, in 1821. Polidori had returned to verse, his first love, and had attempted the monumental task of approaching a subject dealt with by that leading light of English letters, Milton. Indeed, the only reviewer of the poem could not believe that the author had summoned the courage to venture on such a subject. God has entrusted the angels to protect Adam and all accept their task with the exception of one, leading to an angelic rebellion put down by those remaining faithful to God. The resulting punishment condemns the revolutionary angels to a life of mere humanity.

Little remarked upon at the time, subsequent critics have noted the poem's departure from conventional thought – the mocking of God and the angels' punishment as mere mortals thereby awakes a human spirit rather than facing the pits of hell:

> Then sounds alone, like Etna's breathings, broke
> Upon the wilder'd ear of Seraphin,

And seem'd as if the presence they bespoke
Of one who mock'd at God and scoff'd at him.
For element 'gainst element was loudly warring,
And latent flames, and waves, and rocks, were broken jarring;
Then were unknown fair music's magical power,
The still soft sounding of the speaking wave,
The rolling clash of clouds, that profoundly lower
As if the Almighty used the voice they gave.

The poem will never be recognized in the same league as his illustrious contemporaries, Byron and Shelley, but it is remarkable coming from the mind of a man who is struggling with depression and brain damage. John's clipped, aphasic speech was worsening and alarming those around him. It also led him to make some very unwise decisions regarding the company he was keeping.

Gambling is a vice that hardly features in Polidori's diary but it make appearances in both *The Vampyre* and *Ernestus Berchtold*. Ernestus is led down the path of wagering away his money by his friend, Olivieri. The initial winning streaks inevitably turn into heavy losses. In this vignette, Olivieri has introduced Ernestus to an alluring temptress who persuades him to stake his cash:

> Sitting at a window, she drew me into conversation, gradually she approached the table; we at first stood merely as spectators; at last she tempted me to try my fortune: I consented, laid down my stake, it was soon increased to an enormous amount, for I was successful: I threw it into her lap and we parted. For several nights I was equally fortunate; but at length I lost. I was so profusely supplied with money by the kind friend who called me son, that I did not at first heed my losses. I had given all I gained to the syren, who still urged me on: I lost every franc I had.

The perils of gambling were not lost on John, but he failed to heed the moral of his own story. His illustrious nephew, Dante Gabriel Rossetti, the pre-Raphaelite painter and poet, assures us that his uncle would not have succumbed to betting had he been in his right mind. Unfortunately, Polidori was both depressed and desperate enough to make the calamitous decision in the summer of 1821 to head for

Brighton in the company of those who encouraged him to drink and gamble recklessly.

Brighton, at the time, had been made popular by the Prince Regent, later George IV. In 1815, the architect, John Nash, had extended Brighton Pavilion for the Prince and turned it into the elaborate pseudo-Indian sugary confection that we all know today. George was a womanizer, who used the town as a bolt-hole away from the prying eyes of the court, and he was not alone in treating Brighton as a playground. The Pavilion is located in The Steyne area, now known as the Old Steine, which was the social centre for the young Regency buck.

Gambling was rife in the town, especially in aristocratic circles, and rooms were usually set aside for the specific purpose of playing cards. One particularly popular game was faro, which originated in seventeenth century France. It was played using one deck of cards, with a designated banker and a group of players who were known as the punters. A suit of cards was selected and pasted to the table which represented the betting layout. In turn, each player would put a stake on one of these cards and the deck was then placed in a spring-loaded box which would automatically deal cards to supposedly prevent ungentlemanly manipulation. The first drawn banker's card was a losing number and the second drawn player's card represented a winning number. Amounts wagered on neither of these numbers stayed in play for the next round.

Faro is referred to in *The Vampyre* when Aubrey is travelling with Ruthven. He is astounded at the aristocrat's voracious appetite for the game:

> At Brussels and other towns through which they passed, Aubrey was surprised at the apparent eagerness with which his companion sought for the centres of all fashionable vice; there he entered into all the spirit of the faro table. He betted, and always gambled with success, except when the known sharper was his antagonist, and then he lost even more than he gained . . .

The matter of accumulating debt was a very troubling question for participants in games such as faro. The fashion icon and all-round dandy, Beau Brummell, made the decision to exile himself to France when he was unable to cover the amounts he owed. We can see in Brummell's hedonistic round of shopping, riding, gambling at the gentleman's club, theatre visits, more gambling at Almack's Assembly Rooms, whoring and partying, how he may have accumulated frightening debits in his personal accounts. These debts were seen in the Regency era as a matter of honour and were expected to be paid at once. There are many instances of such exile and more than one case that led to an unfortunate suicide.

Brighton remains the playground for Londoners seeking "fashionable vices" in a more conducive atmosphere. It is well-known as 'London by the Sea'. The seafront is still proudly lined by the elegant Georgian mansions that sprang up during the reign of George IV, although many of them have been divided into flats that sell for tidy prices. The plethora of bars, restaurants, and network of lanes lend a trendy air to the more obvious attractions of a seaside resort. The saucy postcard element has been replaced by hipsters and a liberal attitude that has enabled a considerable gay population to make its home in the town.

One of your authors grew up in Brighton and has witnessed its gradual change over recent decades. Fond childhood memories of seaside picnics, riding the pier's ghost train and visits to the archaic dolphinarium, thankfully now obsolete, developed into teenage years of rifling through the fashion and music shops of the Laines and a young adulthood experiencing the town's varied nightlife, little appreciating the wealth of choice and opportunity. Many come in search of these life-affirming benefits but, like Polidori, not all find their expectations realized. Brighton, raised to city status in 2000, is a place of contrast and has some of the most deprived and affluent areas in England. The local paper, *The Argus*, reported a study in 2015 stating that "those living in inner city Brighton and Hove are among the most at risk of crime in the country". However, it should be taken into account that, as with any cosmopolitan hub that offers both shades of darkness and light, if you are searching for trouble, you will be likely to find it; John Polidori certainly did.

Brighton left John not only broken financially but also physically. We imagine him sat at the green baize of a faro table until the early hours of the morning, experiencing an acute loss of vision and blinding headaches, a pain tripled by the steady ebb of his finances. Fair-weather companions must have surrounded him, egging him on to make just one more bet that would solve all his problems and make everything right. He would have drunk to hide the pain, impairing still further his decision making. He returned from Brighton at the end of August in a dangerously weakened state. He had pains in his stomach, even more pressing issues with his vision and fragmented speech that rendered him only partially comprehensible. His godfather, John Deagostini, said that he spoke "in half sentences in conversing on politics and future time".

The house at Great Pulteney Street was empty apart from his godfather and the maid. The most startling aspect of Deagostini's dinner with John was the conversation they had on "future time". John knew that his grains of sand were rapidly running out. He turned to the older man and told Deagostini that his time on earth would be greater than John's own. It is difficult to see this as anything other than a prognosis of his imminent death.

On 24 August 1821, John was found by the maid, Charlotte Read, lying on his bed in a critical state. The night before, he had parted from Deagostini to retire at about nine o'clock, and Charlotte had left a glass tumbler in his room which was not an unusual request; it was rather his state of health that had alarmed her. He had asked Charlotte not to disturb him but, by twelve the next morning when he had not surfaced, she thought it wise to go and open the shutters in order to gently wake him. His condition so greatly upset her that she ran to Deagostini for assistance and then went to seek a doctor.

Two medical men arrived. Thomas Copeland, a surgeon from Golden Square, saw Polidori senseless and dying. He made an attempt to empty John's stomach without success. Another surgeon, William Davis, hurried to the front room of the first floor to find that John had already died. Gaetano and his family, away at their country cottage, were blissfully ignorant of the sad events unfolding in Soho. His father returned several hours after John's passing.

The inquest into Polidori's death was called for the following day and took place in the evening in front of twenty-four local jurors. Details of the inquest are still available and the verdict "departed this Life in a natural way by the Visitation of God" has been the subject of much controversy ever since. There are certain inconsistencies in the witness testimonies; for example, Copeland arrives around one o'clock and finds John dying whereas Davis purports to have arrived between twelve and one and found him already dead. In addition, the maid, Charlotte, states that Polidori was undressed, but Copeland reports that he was clothed. These are mere bagatelles in comparison with the overall verdict of natural death and the perceived wisdom that Polidori committed suicide.

The tumbler that Charlotte had left for John seems to have been a key element. Deagostini noticed the glass when he went into John's room but testifies that it only contained water. He also states that Dr Copeland drank from the tumbler. The assumption has always been that Polidori killed himself with prussic acid, the substance ultimately derived from Konrad Dippel's experiments, and the chemical John had dabbled with in Geneva. The fact that one doctor had tried to empty the contents of his stomach and, rather foolhardily, had drunk from the glass, suggests that suicide was most definitely suspected.

Polidori's relative, William Michael Rossetti, the eventual curator of his diary, is on record as saying that family members were sure he had taken prussic acid in large quantity which would have been fatal. Interestingly, as Franklin Bishop points out, hydrocyanic acid, as it is better known, was used as a sedative when diluted with other liquids and it could have been that John, in his befuddled state, had incorrectly mixed ingredients. There was no sign of a suicide note, merely the prophetic statement John had made the previous evening that his godfather would outlive him. Prussic acid is also very quick to act on the body, and the witness statements are clear in the sense that it took John some time to die.

It is owing to Rossetti's interpretation that pocket biographies of Polidori always point towards his suicide. In the December 1961 edition of the British Medical Journal, a doctor from Boston, Massachusetts, Henry R. Viets, decided a reappraisal of the inquest was

long overdue. He finds the judgement of the coroner's jury to be deci-
sive, given that neither of the two doctors mentioned prussic acid and
that one of the doctors drank from the infamous tumbler – an action
that must have indicated his belief that it was not tainted with poison.
Viets finds the evidence of Polidori's long-lasting nervous instability,
resulting from his head injury, of importance with regard to his death.

For Viets, the most significant factor in ruling out suicide by the popu-
larly accepted means is the time differential between the maid's
discovery and Dr Copeland's arrival:

> The important point is he found Polidori alive. If the maid ran
> to Copeland's house on Golden Square and the doctor came back
> with her on the run, the elapsed time can hardly have been less
> than a half-hour, perhaps longer. Such an interval of time is
> inconsistent with prussic acid as the cause of death.

The only oddity in this chain of events is William Davis' vague approx-
imation of the time that he had arrived at the house. As we know, he
vaguely states any time between twelve and one and that Polidori was
already dead. There was no mention of post mortem examination or,
for that matter, tests on the contents of the glass tumbler. Conclusions
are made simply on testimony. Given the reliance on oral evidence,
what credence do we place on this statement from William Michael
Rossetti?

> On August 1821 he committed suicide with poison – having,
> through losses in gambling, incurred a debt of honour which he
> had no present means of clearing off. That he did take poison,
> prussic acid, was a fact perfectly well known in his family; but it
> is curious to note that the easy-going and good-naturedly
> disposed coroner's jury were content to return a verdict without
> eliciting any distinct evidence as to the cause of death . . .

We could infer from this that Rossetti thought the jury and, for that
matter, the doctors, were kind enough to avoid deeper investigation
that would have seen John interred at a crossroads as a suicide rather
than having a proper Christian burial.

Sifting through the evidence and the interpretations put forward by others, we believe the true catalyst for John's death lies in Costessey Park. The severe cerebral trauma that he sustained is in no doubt responsible for the resulting change in speech patterns, thought processes and behaviour which provide the key to the events of that August. Whether John had gambled heavily or not, it was clear that his health was dramatically declining and the doctor would have administered his own pain relief. The only question that remains is one of intention. Were the combination of gambling debts and severe pain enough to persuade him that life was not worth living or was he just seeking the oblivion of sleep for a few hours? Or, without evidence of prussic acid in the room, did he simply die from the effects of his considerable brain injury?

In the Journal of Neurology, *Brain*, McMillan and Teasdale conducted a study into death rates for head injury published in August 2007, which concluded that there was an increased risk of death for at least seven years after the initial injury. Carried out in Glasgow, the investigation found "for every 10 people aged 15-54 years in the general population in Glasgow who died each year, there were 85 people in this age group who died after head injury" – a significant increase. Notably, some of those who died had epileptic seizures or generalized seizures. Lifestyle also seems to have had an impact. If Polidori had been drinking heavily in Brighton and become stressed through the loss of large amounts of money, this can have only contributed to his deteriorating condition.

Gaetano Polidori was devastated by his son's death and could not talk about the rationale behind it. In a letter written during the following December, he shows the extent of his grief: "I have been left miserable and unhappy for the rest of my life: the idea of not seeing him again, of not hearing his voice any more compared to those times when I used to see and hear him, accompanies me continuously . . . " Harriet Martineau was also affected deeply as her autobiography illustrates: "I was then at the height of my religious fanaticism; and I remember putting away all counts about the theological propriety of what I was doing, for the sake of the relief of praying for his soul." From this statement we can tell she believed Polidori's death to be by his own hand and, indeed, she previously mentions his "gaming debts".

It did not take long for the theory of suicide to run like a hare through literary London. The publisher, John Murray, informed Byron as much, despite the death notice that appeared in *The Traveller* which made no mention of the cause. Byron's friend, Medwin, reports the poet's response, supposedly verbatim:

> I was convinced something very unpleasant hung over me last night; I expected to hear that somebody I knew was dead. So it turns out – poor Polidori is gone. When he was my physician he was always talking of prussic acid, oil of amber, blowing into his veins, suffocating by charcoal, and compounding poisons; but for different purposes to what the Pontic Monarch did, for he has prescribed a dose for himself that would have killed fifty Mithridates – a dose whose effect, Murray says, was so instantaneous, that he went off without a spasm or a struggle. It seems disappointment was the cause of this rash act.

We can already see the distortions in fact beginning to appear, for John's death was not instantaneous and he clung to life for some time.

The most poignant statement regarding the events was issued at the head of a reprinted edition of *The Fall of the Angels* now attributed to its author:

> His father, who was in the country, arrived a few hours after the melancholy event, to hear the dreadful and unexpected news of the death of a beloved son at the age of five and twenty. A Coroner's inquest was held on the ensuing evening, in the presence of a respectable jury composed of about twenty persons, who returned a verdict 'Died by the Visitation of God'. The rest of Dr Polidori's family, who were all in the country, having returned directly, accompanied the deceased on the 29th to his grave, in the Churchyard of St Pancras, where his afflicted parent intends to erect a stone.

Gaetano fulfilled his promise and erected a headstone to his son but John's passage through the realms of death would be as unquiet as his journey through life.

St Pancras Old Church, on London's Pancras Road, dates back to the Norman Conquest. Appropriately for John, today it worships in the Anglo-Catholic tradition of the Church of England where emphasis is placed on the fact that Anglicanism is considered as a branch of the historic Catholic Church rather than a breakaway wing of Protestantism. Worshippers with this belief are sometimes known as Anglican Papalists. Back in the 1860s, the churchyard was threatened by the ever-increasing needs of Victorian railway developers. Scandalous removal of remains and memorials prompted the engagement of an architect to make sure railway expansion was carried out with the necessary delicacy. Arthur Blomfield handed the rather macabre job to minion, Thomas Hardy, then a budding architect who would go on to publish *Far from the Madding Crowd* in 1874.

The grave of Mary Wollstonecraft, Mary Shelley's mother, was spared. This was the spot where Mary and Percy Bysshe had some of their first clandestine assignations. John's remains were not so fortunate and were removed to a mass unmarked burial site. The headstones were gathered and encircle a tree in the graveyard. We went to pay our respects at the foot of what has now become known as the Hardy Tree. The headstones clustered around the base of the venerable ash lack a regimented order, giving them the appearance of having sprung from the tree's roots, cascading out towards the hedge that has been planted around the ensemble.

The close proximity of each headstone to its neighbour has encouraged the growth of moss and lichen, contributing to the obliteration of commemorative inscriptions on the stone. Weathering has also played its part in anonymizing the people once lovingly remembered. John Polidori's headstone may well be sheltering under Hardy's tree but it is impossible to tell. For the man who wrote *The Vampyre*, it is a bitter irony that he was not allowed to rest peacefully in his grave. Even Hardy, repelled by the task, was later moved to write 'The Levelled Churchyard' when the flattening of Wimborne Minster's graves prompted memories of St Pancras.

"O passenger, pray list and catch
Our sighs and piteous groans,

Half stilted in this jumbled patch
Of wretched memorial stones!

"We late-lamented, resting here,
Are mixed to human jam,
And each to each exclaims in fear,
'I know not which I am!' . . .

Polidori, even though he died at such a young age, had achieved so much. His prodigious rise to the title of doctor at a time when most modern-day students would be starting their degree, may have given him false expectations of life. The ability to help one's fellow man through his expertise as a physician was not enough for John. His hankering for literary fame would prove to be his undoing. That he had some talent as a writer has been subsequently recognized by critics, but he did not have the luxury of aristocratic moneyed leisure time to hone the bare bones of his craft. Add to this the uncanny parallel between his father's experience and his own crises in the employ of a famous man and the die was cast. Polidori could never escape the inevitable comparisons between anything he produced and the genius of Byron.

The Vampyre scandal was the wound that cut deepest. Having written a novella that was worthy of publishing, he was once again overshadowed by Byron. We feel compelled to believe John's version of events, but even less biased readers should recognize there is enough room for doubt to excuse Polidori in any culpability. Yet, well into the twentieth century, Byron biographers have unquestioningly pinned the accusation of plagiarism on John's lapel without a second thought.

The few who have written on Polidori's life acknowledge a curious postscript to his death by describing a strange event that took place in the November of 1865. In vogue at the time was the séance and cult of spiritualism. William Michael Rossetti attended one of these esoteric events in north-west London. The medium found herself channelling William's uncle. Of course, Rossetti was keen to ask him how he had died, to which the spirit replied that he had been "killed". When William asked at whose hand, the reply came back, "I". Seemingly, John's ghost identified his connection with Byron via the Ouija board and when asked, "Are you happy?" replied with two knocks implying that this was not exactly the case.

Having walked in John's footsteps, explored the sights at which he had marvelled, and read the words he had committed to his diary, we prefer to end with the championing of his legacy. *The Vampyre*, a genre-creating work, is as much the study of a real-life relationship that had soured, as it is the spawning of a re-invented legend in the person of a cold-hearted aristocrat. His later work shows that he was also trying to move away from the over-excitable pretensions of his youth and who knows what a less frantic maturity would have produced. The most touching dedication of all comes from Christopher Frayling, the academic who compiled the definitive anthology on the subject of the undead:

For Dr John William Polidori,
Who came too close to a vampire.

Bibliography

Andahazi, Federico. *The Merciful Women* (New York: Grove Press, 2000).

Baedeker, Karl. *Switzerland and the Adjacent Portions of Italy, Savoy and the Tyrol* (Leipzig: Baedeker, 1887).

Beattie, Andrew. *The Alps: A Cultural Guide* (Oxford: Signal Books, 2006).

Bishop, Franklin. *Polidori!: A Life of Dr John Polidori* (Chislehurst: The Gothic Society at Gargoyle's Head Press, 1991).

Boccaccio, Giovanni. *Elegia di Madonna Fiammetta* (Milan, Mursia, 1987).

Byron, George Gordon. *Poetical Works* (Oxford: Oxford University Press, 1967).

Carrère, Emmanuel. *Gothic Romance* (New York: Scribner, 1990).

Chaucer, Geoffrey. *The Canterbury Tales* (London: Penguin, 20015).

Cheetham, Simon. *Byron in Europe* (Wellingborough: Equation, 1988).

Cochran, Peter (ed.). *Hobhouse's Diary* (petercochran.wordpress.com/hobhouses-diary/, 2016).

Coleridge, Samuel Taylor. *The Rime of the Ancient Mariner and Other Poems* (Mineola: Dover Publications, 1992).

Coryate, Thomas. *Coryat's Crudities hastily gobbled up in five moneths' travells* (London: W. Cater, 1776).

Dunsterville, Augusta. *La Genève de Victor Frankenstein* (Geneva: Fondation Martin Bodmer, 2016).

Eisler, Benita. *Byron: Child of Passion, Fool of Fame* (London: Penguin, 2000).

Florescu, Radu. *In Search of Frankenstein* (London: New English Library, 1977).

Frayling, Christopher. *Vampyres: Lord Byron to Count Dracula* (London: Faber and Faber, 1992).

Gordon, Charlotte. *Romantic Outlaws: The Extraordinary Lives of Mary Wollstonecraft and Mary Shelley* (London: Windmill Books, 2016).

Grattan, Thomas Colley. *Lays and Legends of the Rhine* (Frankfurt: Charles Jugel, 1847).

Hancock, Albert Elmer. *The French Revolution and the English Poets: A Study in Historical Criticism* (New York: Henry Holt and Company, 1899).

Hardy, Thomas. *Poems of Thomas Hardy* (London: Macmillan, 1974).

Hay, Daisy. *Young Romantics* (London: Bloomsbury, 2011).

Holmes, Richard. *Shelley: The Pursuit* (London: Penguin, 1987).

Hoobler, Dorothy & Hoobler, Thomas. *The Monsters* (New York: Little, Brown & Co, 2006).

Horton, Alice (tr.). *The Lay of the Nibelungs* (London: George Bell and Sons, 1901).

Koch, Peter. *John Lloyd Stephens and Frederick Catherwood: Pioneers of Mayan Archaeology* (Jefferson: McFarland and Company, 2013).

Lewis, Matthew. *The Monk* (Oxford: Oxford University Press, 2008).

Longford, Elizabeth. *Byron* (London: Hutchinson, 1976).

MacCarthy, Fiona. *Byron: Life and Legend* (London: John Murray, 2014).

MacDonald, David Lorne. *Poor Polidori: A Critical Biography* (Toronto: University of Toronto Press, 1991).

Markovits, Benjamin. *Imposture* (London: Faber and Faber, 2007).

Martineau, Harriet. *Autobiography Volume I* (Boston: James R. Osgood & Co, 1877).

McConnell Stott, Andrew. *The Vampyre Family* (Edinburgh: Canongate, 2013).

McMillan, T. M. and Teasdale, G. M. 'Death rate is increased for at least 7 years after head injury: a prospective study', *Brain*, Vol. 130, No. 10 (Oxford University Press, 2007).

Meeres, Frank. *Strangers: A History of Norwich's Incomers* (Norwich: Norwich Heritage Economic and Regeneration Trust, 2012).

Melville, Herman. *Pierre: or, The Ambiguities* (New York, Harper and Brothers, 1852).

Moore, Thomas. *Life of Lord Byron Vol. III with his Letters and Journals* (London: John Murray, 1851).

Müller, Wolfgang. *Dichtungen eines rheinischen Poeten* (Leipzig: Brodhaus, 1871).

Murray, John (ed.). *A Handbook for Travellers on the Continent* (London: John Murray, 1845).

Ospina, William. *El año del verano que nunca llegó* (Mexico City: Random House, 2015).

Patané, Vincenzo. *L'estate di un ghiro: il mito di Lord Byron* (Venice: Cicero, 2013).

Paterson (ed.). *Guide to the Rhine and its Provinces* (London: Oliphant, Anderson & Ferrier, 1886).

Polidori, John William. *The Vampyre and Other Writings* (Manchester: Fyfield Books, 2005).

Polidori, John William & Bridgens, Richard. *Sketches Illustrative of the Manners and Costumes of France, Switzerland, and Italy* (London: Hatchard & Son, 1821).

Polidori, John William & Rossetti, William Michael. *The Diary of Dr. John William Polidori 1816 relating to Byron, Shelley etc.* (Cambridge: Cambridge University Press, 2014).

Quennell, Peter. *The Years of Fame – Byron in Italy* (Glasgow: Collins, 1974).

Raphael, Frederic. *Byron* (London: Thames and Hudson, 1982).

Reichard, Heinrich. *Guide des Voyageurs en Europe* (Weimar: Bureau d'Industrie, 1805).

Rieger, James. 'Dr. Polidori and the Genesis of Frankenstein', *Studies in English Literature, 1500–1900*, Vol. 3, No. 4 (Rice University, 1963).

Rigby, Mair. '"Prey to some cureless disquiet": Polidori's Queer Vampyre at the Margins of Romanticism', *Romanticism on the Net* (http://id.erudit.org/iderudit/011135ar, November 2004).

Robberds, John Warden. *A Memoir of the Life and Writings of the Late William Taylor of Norwich Volume I* (London: John Murray, 1843).

Roche, Tony. 'Le centenaire de Byron à Genèva', *L'Impartial*, 6th May, 1924.

Rodenbach, Georges. *Bruges-la-Morte* (Sawtry: Dedalus, 2009).

Rousseau, Jean-Jacques. *The Confessions of Jean-Jacques Rousseau* (Mineola: Dover Publications, 2014).

Rowe, Richard Paul. *The Shakespeare Guide to Italy* (London: Harper Perennial, 2011).

Scarpa, Tiziano. *Venice is a Fish: A Cultural Guide* (London: Serpent's Tail, 2009).

Sealts, Merton. *Melville's Reading* (Columbia: University of South Carolina Press, 1989).

Shelley, Mary. *Frankenstein* (Oxford: Oxford University Press, 2009).

Shelley, Mary. *History of a Six Weeks' Tour* (London: Hookham & Ollier, 1817).

Shelley, Percy Bysshe. *The Selected Poetry and Prose of Shelley* (Ware: Wordsworth Editions, 2002).

Smithers, Henry. *Observations Made During a Tour in 1816 and 1817* (Brussels: 1818).

Snowe, Joseph. *The Rhine, Legends, Traditions, History, from Cologne to Mainz* (London: F. C. Westley, 1839).

Southey, Robert. *The Poetical Works of Robert Southey* (London: Longman, Brown, Green and Longmans, 1850).

Twain, Mark. *A Tramp Abroad* (London: Chatto and Windus, 1889).

Vincent, Patrick (ed.). *Chillon: A Literary Guide* (Geneva: Fondation du Cháteau de Chillon, 2010).

West, Paul. *Lord Byron's Doctor* (London: Serpent's Tail, 1992).

Index